Beyond El Dorado
power and gold
in ancient Colombia

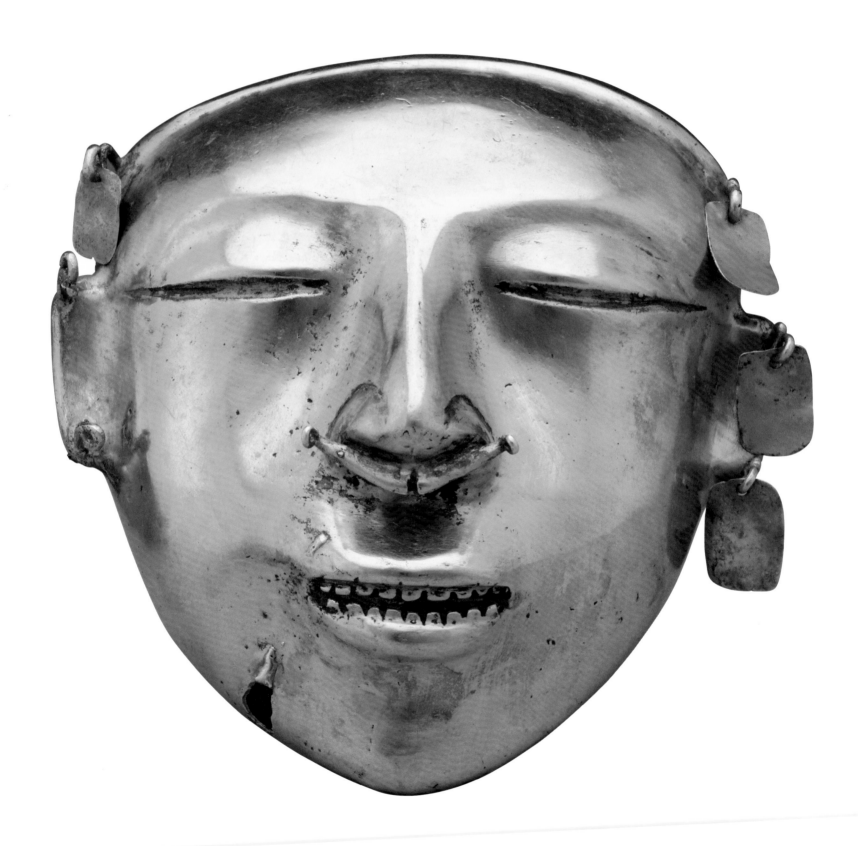

Elisenda
Vila Llonch

Beyond El Dorado
power and gold in ancient Colombia

An exhibition organized with
the Museo del Oro, Colombia

The British Museum

This book is published to accompany the exhibition
Beyond El Dorado: power and gold in ancient Colombia at
the British Museum 17 October 2013–23 March 2014.

The exhibition is sponsored by Julius Baer.
Additional support provided by American Airlines.

American Airlines

© 2013 The Trustees of the British Museum

First published in 2013 by The British Museum Press
A division of the British Museum Company Ltd
38 Russell Square, London WC1B 3QQ
britishmuseum.org/publishing

A catalogue record for this book is available from
the British Library

ISBN 978 0 7141 2541 1

Designed by Zach John Design
Printed in Italy by Graphicom srl

The papers used by The British Museum Press are
recyclable products and the manufacturing processes
are expected to conform to the environmental regulations
of the country of origin.

Half-title page: Lime dipper
(see p. 139)
Frontispiece: Mask pectoral
(see p. 39)
Opposite: Crocodile-shaped
pendant (see p. 147)

Contents

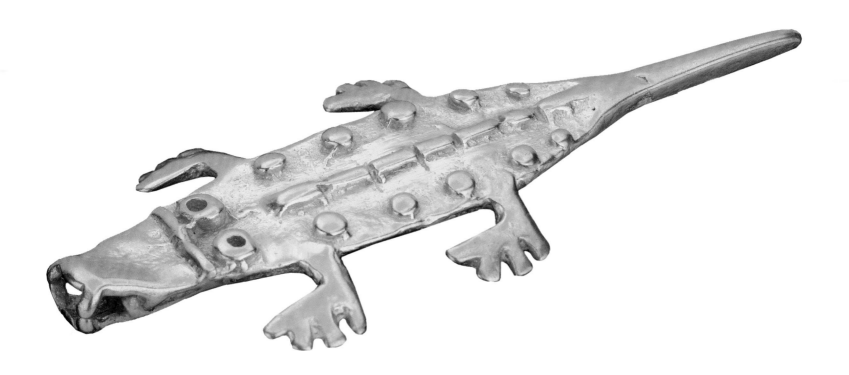

Bird-shaped staff finial
200 BC – AD 1000
Early Zenú
Gold alloy
H 4.5 cm, W 2.7 cm,
L 10.5 cm
Museo del Oro (O33449)

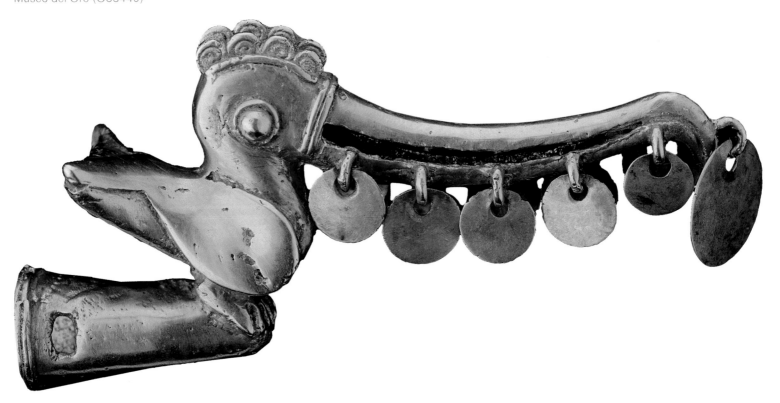

Museo del Oro Director's Foreword

Colombia's Banco de la República Gold Museum is home to one of the most important collections of pre-Hispanic metalwork in the world. The Museum undertakes research and makes its collection known, so that it can be a source of knowledge, inspiration and enjoyment for present and future generations of Colombians. Through exhibitions and activities at its headquarters in Bogotá and its six regional museums, the Gold Museum fulfils its mission with children, adults, students, researchers, and many other population groups over a wide area of the country. The collection of pre-Hispanic metalwork that the Museum has built up and preserved over a period of almost seventy-five years has thus become an essential component of Colombian identity, part of our heritage that fills us with pride and links us to our past, while at the same time providing a foundation that will mark out our future.

The Gold Museum has also played a notable role in representing Colombia abroad, through more than two hundred international exhibitions at widely acclaimed museums, and has given the world the opportunity to explore and enjoy this outstanding cultural inheritance. As a result of this international exhibition programme, large numbers of people from all around the globe have been able to appreciate the skill, spiritual meaning and technological complexity of the objects made of gold and gold alloys by indigenous societies in Colombia over a period stretching back more than two thousand years, and to accept those objects as part of the heritage of all mankind.

The Banco de la República Gold Museum has great pleasure in exhibiting this select sample of pre-Hispanic indigenous art. Amazingly, these objects from the past have the power to teach us and to inspire us today to find alternative, more viable ways of thinking about our place in the world and how we relate to each other and to our environment. On behalf of Banco de la República, I would like to thank Director Neil MacGregor and his staff for the warm welcome we have received at the British Museum.

María Alicia Uribe
Director
Museo del Oro - Banco de la República
Colombia

British Museum Director's Foreword

The people of ancient Colombia are most famous today for their gold: that fame was summed up in the European myth of El Dorado, 'the golden one', which imagined fabulous wealth waiting to be found in the peaks and plains of the northern Andes. Indeed, in the towns, villages, fields and burial places of the region, many gold objects were to be found. But these intricate and technically sophisticated gold objects meant more to their makers and users than wealth alone. In several senses these objects were made as a means of connecting with the complex spiritual realm that the people of the region inhabited before the arrival of the Europeans.

This book and the exhibition it accompanies move beyond the myth of El Dorado to explore these remarkable societies through the gold, the ceramics and the other kinds of objects that they made and which remain today to represent them. There were in the region more than thirty different societies: while they traded ideas and objects with each other, each had a distinct character and artistic style. They also traded gold itself: as a raw material it occurred only in some areas. Goldsmiths carefully used this raw material, mixing the silver-bearing gold with copper to create alloys with distinctive properties. They valued the transformations in the quality of gold that they were able to create, and the transformations in the spiritual realm that these objects assisted and simultaneously represented.

This collaboration between the Museo del Oro, Bogota and the British Museum enables us to think about the meaning of gold and other materials in these ancient societies and indeed in our own. We are delighted to work with the Museo del Oro on this project. Staging exhibitions on this scale is simply not possible without external support and we are extremely grateful for the generosity of Julius Baer for sponsoring the exhibition and also to our airline partner American Airlines.

Studying these societies enables us to move beyond the idea of El Dorado as merely a dream of wealth, to a wider understanding of value, and values, within society – and to the ways in which spiritual and social concepts can be given material form.

Neil MacGregor
Director
The British Museum

Sponsor's Foreword

Julius Baer's long standing tradition of delivering quality private banking is strengthened by our promise to also deliver social and economic returns. We are the leading private banking group in Switzerland which will incorporate a large footprint in the UK. Our presence in Europe spans decades, as does our responsibility to the communities where we do business.

Our corporate philosophy is extensive, and our affinity with the world of art and culture is just one of many pillars in which we invest our time and resources. This ethos is also reflected by our global sponsorship strategy, which includes cultural commitments in the fields of art and classical music and several other areas.

Delivering outstanding performances is a shared goal that can inspire both artists and economists alike. At Julius Baer our commitment is to make this inspiration accessible to all. Art is a universal language, bringing people together from all backgrounds, connecting them in a way that few other experiences can.

Sponsoring the British Museum has allowed Julius Baer the privilege of working with one of the UK's most outstanding institutions whose reputation in showing exhibitions of this kind is internationally recognised. We are proud to be the sponsor of *Beyond El Dorado: power and gold in ancient Colombia*, which provides a unique insight into the cultural richness of pre-Hispanic Colombia.

I hope this book inspires you and brings about a deeper understanding of the diverse world we share.

Gian A. Rossi

Head Northern, Central and Eastern Europe
Member of the Executive Board
Bank Julius Baer & Co. Ltd.

Julius Bär

											Muisca						Muisca
									Nahuange			Tairona					Tairona
							Early Period				Late Period						Zenú
					Early Period					Late Period							Quimbaya
		Early Period				Middle Period					Late Period						Tolima
llama											Yotoco						Calima

| 1600 BC | 1400 BC | 1200 BC | 1000 BC | 800 BC | 600 BC | 400 BC | 200 BC | 0 | AD 200 | AD 400 | AD 600 | AD 800 | AD 1000 | AD 1200 | AD 1400 | AD 1600 |

CARIBBEAN SEA

N

0   300 Miles

0   500 Kilometres

PACIFIC

OCEAN

PANAMA

VENEZUELA

ZENÚ

TAIRONA

Dabeiba

Buriticá

QUIMBAYA

Lake Guatavita

Bogotá

MUISCA

CALIMA-
MALAGANA

TOLIMA

COLOMBIA

TIERRADENTRO

SAN AGUSTÍN

ANDES

EQUADOR

BRAZIL

PERU

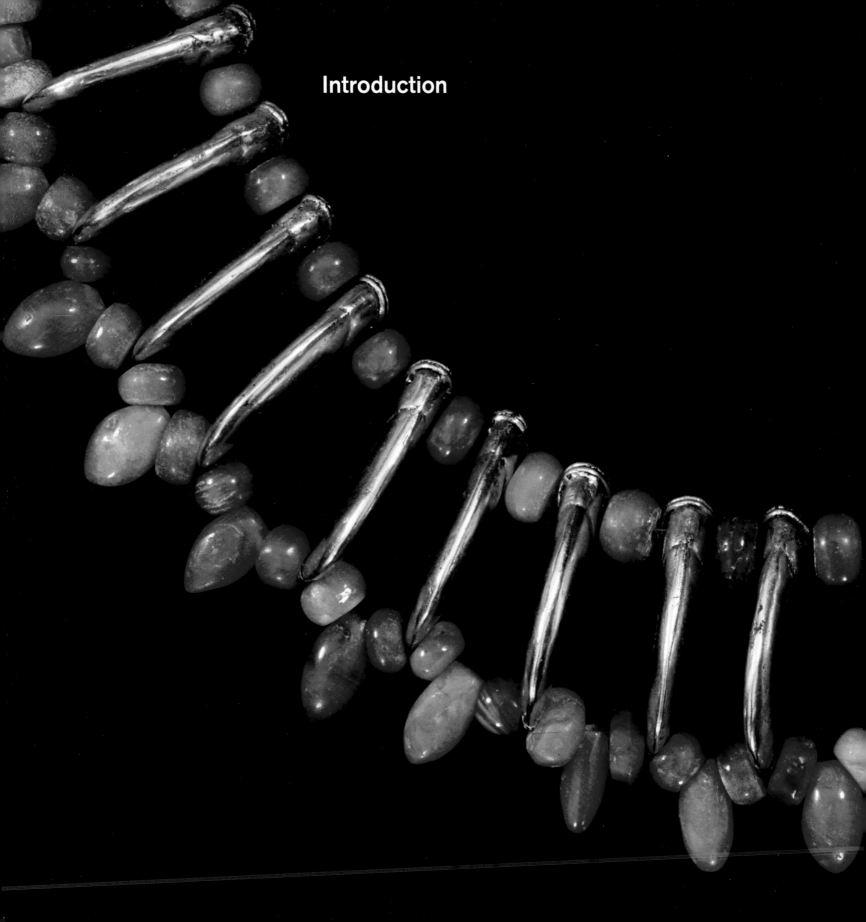

Introduction

Introduction

The ancient Colombians made many different kinds of beautiful and technically complex objects, including textiles and feather ornaments, stone carvings, ceramics and goldwork. Those people and their societies are long gone, but many objects made of stone, ceramic and gold have survived them. Of these, the gold has up to now attracted the most interest. Ancient Colombian goldwork represents one of the most technologically advanced and artistically developed cultural traditions of the Americas. It is also important from the point of view of research: even the little we now know about the original meanings and significance of these objects can significantly alter our understanding of the value and power of gold in ancient Colombia.

Early Spanish explorers of this region brought back to Europe fabulous tales of gold, encapsulated in the story of El Dorado, 'the golden one' (see below). From the 1530s the region attracted many treasure seekers; in their eagerness to obtain gold they paid scant attention to the objects into which it was fashioned. They had no interest in how or why such items were crafted, or in the archaeological contexts in which they were found: treasure seekers looted burial mounds and often melted down the gold items that they found. *Beyond El Dorado* explores the story of ancient Colombia – a series of remarkable societies whose skills and beliefs are still now only partially understood. The knowledge that we have accrued about these societies and the objects they made comes from four main sources: the writings and drawings made by early Spanish chroniclers; more recent archaeological research; analogies made with indigenous Colombian societies today; and studies of the material properties of the objects themselves, now located in museums such as the Museo del Oro in Bogotá.

With the assistance of all these resources, it is possible to study an object such as the pectoral illustrated here to illuminate and further understand the richness and complexity of ancient Colombian societies. This pectoral – an ornament worn on the chest – depicts a decorated human figure that is wearing an elaborate headdress, large nose ring and other kinds of adornment, accompanied by pairs of bird-like attendants. The pectoral was found in the 1930s in a tomb in La Marquesa, Timbío, in the Cauca region of southern Colombia. The tomb comprised a shaft with a side chamber at the bottom. Pectorals such as this have also been found in other tombs, placed on the chest of the deceased.

Pectoral
AD 900–1600
Late Cauca
Gold alloy
H 30 cm, W 20.5 cm
The British Museum
(AM1938,0706.1)

A number of distinct cultures existed in what is now modern-day Colombia, each with different histories and each located in a separate area – now identified as archaeological regions. At the time of European conquest, there were twelve major societies practising metallurgy, of which six are explored here – those we know as Tairona, Tolima, Zenú, Quimbaya, Muisca and Calima. These different societies were known to each other, and valued resources such as shells, feathers and salt were traded between them. Not only were gold objects often traded over long distances, but goldsmiths themselves were also mobile, sometimes working far from their homeland. As a result, objects sometimes appear to incorporate elements of different regional styles. This pectoral, for example, which comes from the Cauca region, shares many features with other styles from the headwater region of the Magdalena and Cauca Rivers.

As most of the pieces created in ancient Colombia, the pectoral is made from an alloy known as *tumbaga* that combines gold and copper as well as some traces of the naturally occurring silver in gold. The metalworkers of this region carefully mixed different degrees of gold and copper to create alloys with specific colours and smells. *Tumbaga* has a lower melting point and is easier to cast than gold alone. It reproduces fine decorative details more easily and it is also a harder material. Gold was mined by various techniques from sources mainly in the Andean cordillera and was traded between the several societies of the region. Metalworking skills and techniques had developed in what is now Bolivia and the southern Andean regions of Peru as early as 2155 BC, and reached the north of the continent about 2500 years ago. Goldsmiths in the Colombian region used a diversity of techniques, including hammering and lost-wax casting (see pp. 55 and 70), to create complex objects. This pectoral was made using both techniques: the figure was cast and the crescent blade under the figure was finished by hammering.

There are a number of pectorals from the Cauca region that resemble this one. Sometimes the figure has a bird's beak rather than a nose, and they are commonly accompanied by small and fabulous animals (see p. 151). They all have a forked headdress as here, interpreted as representing feathers, while the crescent blade beneath the figure has been associated with the spread tail of a bird of prey such as an eagle. The figure shows bindings, both below the knees and in the wrists – a common type of body decoration in these cultures. The large central figure is accompanied by four identical bird-like figures (at its ears and feet) that have beaks and folded wings, as well as two fabulous creatures with bird's heads, and the legs and tail of a monkey. This Cauca pectoral seems to represent a person transformed into a bird of prey.

Drawing on both early Spanish accounts and evidence from indigenous societies in Colombia today, it is often proposed that figures such as this represent people embarking on spiritual journeys and being transformed into birds. Evidence suggests that in the past, as sometimes still today, people in this region did not make much distinction between humans and other natural entities. Instead, humans, animals, birds, plants, rocks and other natural features were all believed to have souls. Each type of person had a way of viewing the world, which was determined by its body, and that body was something that the person could put on and take off. In that sense, the process of a human dressing as a bird was transformative, enabling him to alter his view of the world.

The association between intoxicants, transformation, transfiguration and supernatural spiritual power is strong. There are many objects from the pre-Hispanic period connected with the use of mind-altering substances, including stimulants from plants such as tobacco, coca, *yage/yajé* and *yopo*. Such intoxicants alter the senses and perceptions, and can create an impression of the spirit leaving the body and rising – taking flight like a bird – or of obtaining other animal properties such as night vision. A Muisca priest told an early Spanish visitor that, under the influence of *yopo*, he flew from the village of Ubaque to Santa Marta – a long distance – returning the same night. Cauca pectorals like the one illustrated are often understood to represent a person making such a journey. Much of the art of ancient Colombia suggests this concept of transformation. Objects seem either to represent people dressed as an animal, or perhaps the ability to transform temporarily into that animal. The characteristics of objects from different societies suggest that certain animals held particular significance: bats, birds and jaguars all appear, as do lobsters, snakes, frogs, crocodiles and monkeys. In contemporary indigenous communities, the jaguar is particularly important: it is considered to be both a guardian spirit and an animal into which people can transform themselves.

Societies across this region valued the aesthetic of iridescence, reflection and lustre; they made objects that were highly burnished and polished, or whose surfaces were treated by techniques such as depletion gilding (see p. 56). The use of suspended additions is common to many metalwork pieces: discs and other plates, which were able to move independently, were hung from the main body of the pieces. Such objects probably made a tinkling sound, but also, importantly, would have reflected light, creating flashes when worn, for example, by dancers illuminated by firelight or in the bright sunlight. Such flashes of light and their accompanying sounds would have transformed the everyday, enhancing the possibilities of engagement with the spiritual realm.

Lake Guatavita, Colombia.

Many of the gold objects known today from the region were found, like this pectoral, in tombs. A number of different forms of burial were employed across the region, but generally speaking the dead were interred with objects; elites especially were buried with lavish accompaniments of gold, ceramics and other items including seashells, spindle whorls, stone axes and textiles. In 1554 Pedro de Cieza de León commented that 'the Indians were buried with as much wealth as possible'. When Pedro de Heredia travelled to the Zenú region in 1534, he reported visiting a large town with big houses and a central temple. Around the temple were the burial mounds of leaders, each one topped by a tree whose branches were hung with golden bells.[1]

It was such fabulous tales of gold which the first explorers and colonizers of Colombia took back to Europe that fuelled the gold rush of European occupation. These stories reached their zenith in the elaboration of one specific story: the legend of El Dorado. El Dorado can be translated as 'the gilded one' or 'the golden one' and it was this precious metal that interested those early visitors the most. Indeed, the search for gold was the official objective of the European exploration of this territory; in 1513 the Spanish king Fernando de Aragon ordered the governorship of the region to be called 'Castilla del Oro' (see map overleaf).

The Spanish chronicler Fernández de Oviedo makes the first written

1. Cited in Bray 1978, p. 41.

reference to El Dorado in his *Historia general y natural de las Indias* (1535–48). In this account Oviedo describes a 'golden king', an individual who 'went about all covered with powdered gold, as casually as if it were powdered salt'. This story of a golden ruler was elaborated to become the legend of a 'golden city' or 'golden kingdom' that had endless supplies of gold. European explorers and adventurers, including Sir Walter Raleigh, set out in search of this mythical place.

Oviedo's account was based on a specific ritual of the Muisca people that took place at Lake Guatavita, a circular lake surrounded by steep hills in the crater of an extinct volcano. A range of practices may have taken place in this lake, including those concerned with agricultural cycles of sowing and harvest, and possibly also the movement of the stars. This was not the only such ritual that took place in Muisca lakes and throughout the region – the Muisca revered at least five lakes which were all centres of pilgrimage – but none captured the Spanish imagination to such an extent. During one of the ceremonies a Muisca leader was said to be covered in gold dust from head to toe and borne on a raft into the centre of the lake accompanied by attendants. Once there, the ruler and his attendants threw offerings of gold, emeralds and other items into the depths of the lake.

For the Muisca, the principal importance of gold was as an offering: more than half of Muisca gold production consisted of votive offerings to be buried at special locations such as lakes and caves to restore the equilibrium of the cosmos. According to Muisca thinking, the opposing principles that made up the world (such as man and woman, day and night), needed to be kept at an equilibrium that was ultimately controlled by the gods. When the world was out of balance (when there was no rain, for example) people could intervene by making gifts to the gods asking them to redress the balance of nature.

The Muisca gold objects that were made as votive offerings are figurines known as *tunjos*. Made to be placed throughout the landscape, these images are often roughly finished: the subject matter of *tunjos* was clearly more important than the quality of their workmanship.[2] They are generally made by the lost-wax technique, with a flat plaque on which details were modelled in wax wire and later cast in *tumbaga*. While the modelling is simple, detail is faithfully rendered: *tunjos* illustrate people carrying children, and holding shields, weapons, musical instruments and other everyday objects, so that, like no other art style from the region, they tell us about the life of individuals in Muisca society.[3] The most famous *tunjo* known to us today, now in the Museo del Oro in Bogotá, was found in a cave near Bogotá inside a clay container (see p. 24). It represents an important personage standing on a raft, surrounded by smaller

2. As the archaeologist Warwick Bray has observed. Bray 1978, p. 48.

3. Bray 1978, p. 48.

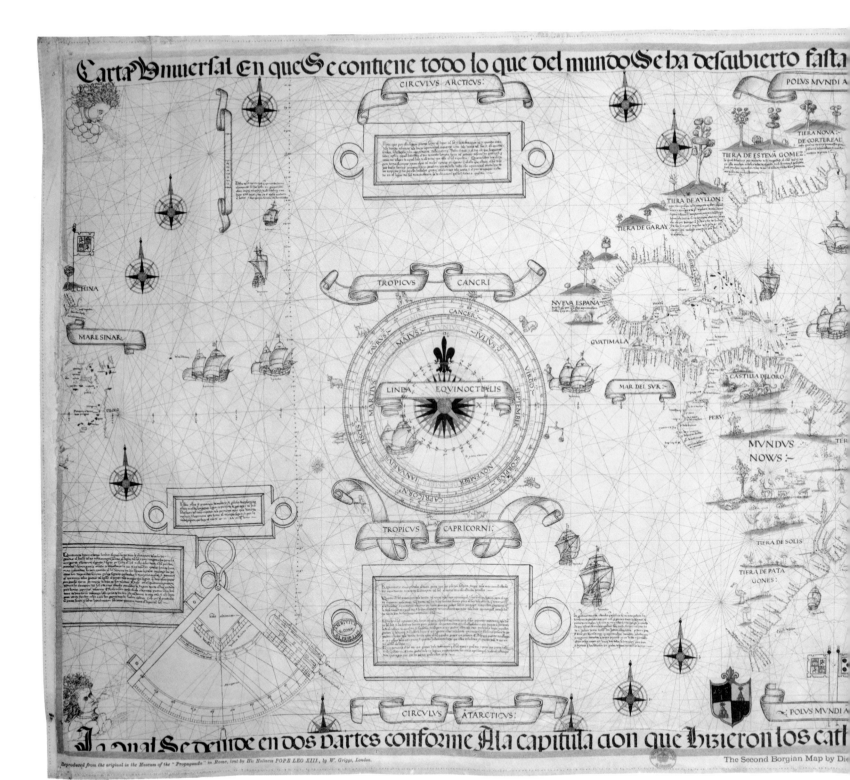

Carta Vniuerfal En que Se contiene todo lo que del mundo Se ha defcubierto fasta

CIRCVLVS ARCTICVS:

POLVS MVNDI A

TIERA NOVA
DE CORTEREAL

TIERA DE ESTEVA GOMEZ:

FLORIDA

TIERA DE AYLLON:

TIERA DE GARAY

CHINA

TROPICVS   CANCRI

NVEVA ESPAÑA

MARE SINAR

GVATIMALA

CANCER

TAVRVS   IVLIVS

MAIVS   VIRGO

MAR DEL SVR

CASTILLA DELORO

LINEA   EQVINOCTIALIS

PERV

SEPTEMBER

ARIES

PISCES   X

MVNDVS
NOWS:

MARTIVS

TER

IANVARI   NOVEMBER

OCTOVS

CAPRICORN

TROPICVS   CAPRICORNI:

TIERA DE SOLIS

TIERA DE PATA
GONES:

CIRCVLVS   ATARCTICVS:

POLVS MVNDI A

Ja qual Se deuide en dos partes conforme Ala capitula aon que hizieron los cat

The Second Borgian Map by Die

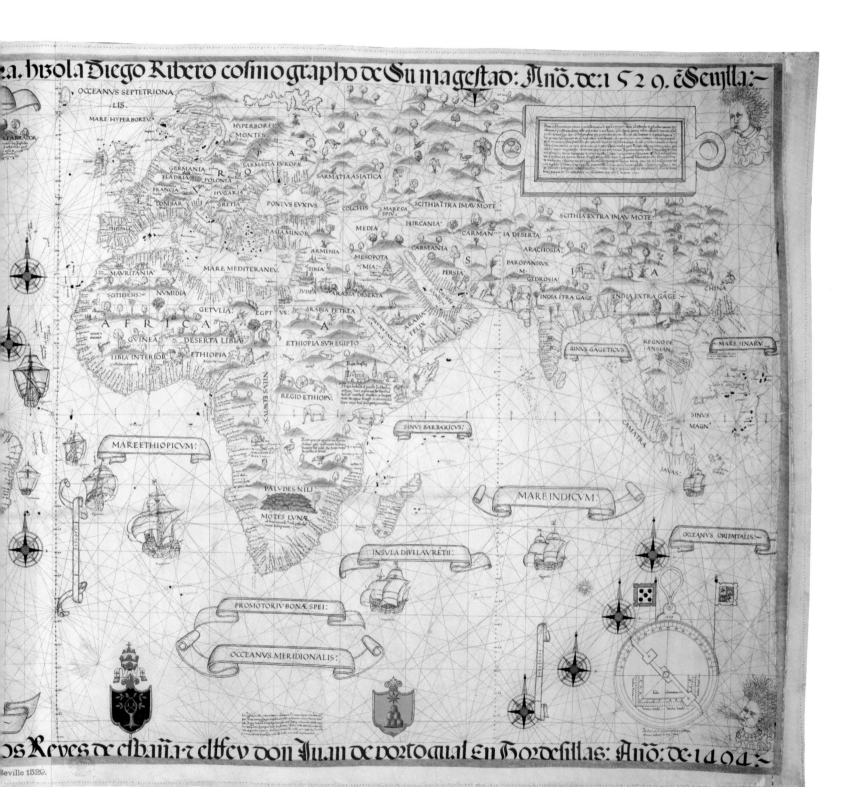

a. hizo la Diego Ribero cofmographo de Su magestad: Anõ. de: 1 5 2 9. é Seuilla:-

os Reyes de eſpaña: z el Rey don Juan de portogual En Hordesillas: Anõ: de 1 4 9 4:-

Seville 1529.

Right: First published illustration of Lake Guatavita from Humbold and Bonpland's *Vue des Cordillères*, 1813. It shows the notch cut at the rim of the lake by Antonio de Sepúlveda in the 1580s in an attempt to drain the lake.

Opposite: An imagined scene of 'The Golden Man'. Engraving by Theodor de Bry, 1599.

figures. The central figure, represented in larger scale and presumably a leader, is adorned with a headdress with dangling plates, nose ornament and other accoutrements. It may be that this image represents the same ceremony that the Spanish chroniclers described.

The most complete account of the Muisca ritual in Lake Guatavita was written by the Bogotá-born Juan Rodríguez Freyle in 1636.[4] It incorporates some misconceptions about the ritual, but is still vivid in its detail. Freyle described how, before it commenced, the leader spent some time secluded in a cave, without women, and forbidden from eating salt and chilli pepper, or going out into the daylight. After this,

The first journey he had to make was to go to the great lagoon of Guatavita, to make offerings and sacrifices to the demon which they worshipped as their god and lord. During the ceremony, which took place at the lagoon, they made a raft of rushes, embellishing and decorating it with the most attractive things they had. They put on it four lighted braziers in which they burned much *moque*, which is the incense of these natives, and also resin and many other perfumes. The lagoon was large and deep, so that a ship with high sides could sail on it, all loaded with an infinity of men and women dressed in fine plumes, golden plaques and crowns.... As soon as those on

4. Freyle named his friend Don Juan, nephew of the last independent lord of Guatavita, as his source for this account.

Raft *tunjo* (votive offering)
AD 600–1600
Muisca
Gold alloy
H 10.2 cm, W 10 cm, L 19.5 cm
Museo del Oro (O11373)

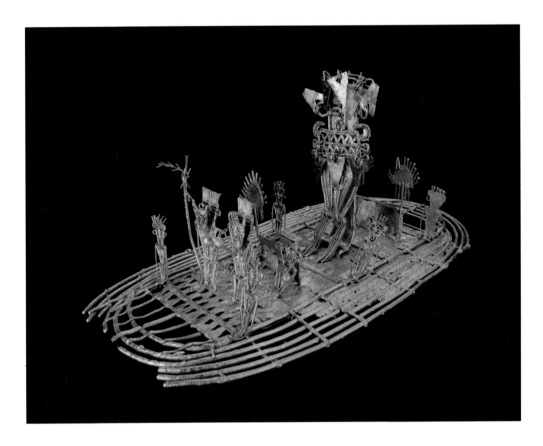

the raft began to burn incense, they also lit braziers on the shore, so that the smoke hid the light of day.

At this time, they stripped the heir to his skin, and anointed him with a sticky earth on which they placed gold dust so that he was completely covered with this metal. They placed him on the raft, on which he remained motionless, and at his feet they placed a great heap of gold and emeralds for him to offer to his god. On the raft with him went four principal subject chiefs, decked in plumes, crowns, bracelets, pendants and earrings all of gold. They, too, were naked, and each one carried his offering. As the raft left the shore the music began, with trumpets, flutes and other instruments, and with singing which shook the mountains and valleys, until, when the raft reached the centre of the lagoon, they raised a banner as a signal for silence.

The gilded Indian then made his offering, throwing out all the pile of gold into the middle of the lake, and the chiefs who had accompanied

Sale catalogue, December 1911, which includes objects excavated from Lake Guatavita in 1910. Some of the pieces in the sale are now in the British Museum collection (see pp. 26–9).

CATALOGUE
OF
ANTIQUE GOLD ORNAMENTS
and Pottery
RECOVERED FROM LAKE GUATAVITA, IN THE REPUBLIC OF
COLOMBIA, SOUTH AMERICA.
DURING THE OPERATIONS OF
"CONTRACTORS LTD." OF 65, LONDON WALL, E.C.

AND OTHER PROPERTIES
INCLUDING
A PAIR OF EGYPTIAN GOLD BRACELETS,
AN ANTIQUE MARBLE BUST OF SENECA,
ANTIQUE GOLD RINGS AND ROMANO-SYRIAN GLASS.

WHICH WILL BE SOLD BY AUCTION,
BY MESSRS.
SOTHEBY, WILKINSON & HODGE
Auctioneers of Literary Property & Works illustrative of the Fine Arts,
AT THEIR HOUSE, No. 13, WELLINGTON STREET, STRAND, W.C.
On MONDAY, the 11th of DECEMBER, 1911,
AT ONE O'CLOCK PRECISELY.

MAY BE VIEWED TWO DAYS PRIOR.   CATALOGUES MAY BE HAD.
DRYDEN PRESS: J. DAVY AND SONS, 8-9, FRITH-STREET, SOHO-SQUARE, W.

him did the same on their own accounts. After this they lowered the flag, which had remained up during the whole time of offering, and, as the raft moved towards the shore, the shouting began again, with pipes, flutes, and large teams of singers and dancers. With this ceremony the new ruler was received, and was recognized as lord and king. From this ceremony came the celebrated name of El Dorado, which has cost so many lives.[5]

As a result of such stories, several attempts have been made to drain Lake Guatavita to retrieve the fabled treasures. Gold, stone beads and ceramics were found but never the riches believed to be buried there. The early emphasis on gold, specifically on El Dorado, has meant that many of the other remarkable features of ancient Colombian societies – their agricultural structures and techniques, their architecture, their ceramics, textiles and other object types – have been overlooked. Today, evidence about such features is hard to obtain and yet, by bringing together what we do know, it is possible to understand at least something of the skills, aesthetic sensibility, beliefs and achievements of the remarkable societies of ancient Colombia. The Cauca pectoral embodies the achievement of pre-Columbian craftsmanship in the Americas. It is this story of value and power – beyond the story of El Dorado – that this book explores.

5. Freyle 1636.

Fragment with four figures
AD 600–1600
Muisca
Ceramic
H 14.5 cm, D 15 cm
The British Museum
(Am1911,1213.11)

Fragment head
AD 600–1600
Muisca
Ceramic
H 19 cm, W 12 cm, D 10.5 cm
The British Museum
(Am1911,1213.2)

**Votive offerings from
Lake Guatavita**

These ceramic figures –
some human, some part
animal – and the stone
beads illustrated overleaf
come from an attempt in
1909 by a British company
to drain the water of Lake
Guatavita, through a
tunnel excavated under
the lake. The pieces show
that Muisca people made
offerings not just of gold, but
of other objects that held
ritual significance.

Figurine
AD 600–1600
Muisca
Ceramic
H 12.5 cm, W 9 cm, D 10 cm
The British Museum
(Am1911,1213.10)

Tripod figurine
Muisca
AD 600–1600
Ceramic
H 17 cm, W 9 cm, D 7 cm
The British Museum
(Am1911,1213.4)

COLOMBIA.
POTTERY VASE FOR GOLD DUST,
FROM THE SACRED LAKE OF
GUATABITA.
Given by Louis Clarke, Esq., 1911.

Necklace
AD 900–1600
Lake Guatavita
Stone
L 56 cm, Diam. 2 cm
The British Museum
(Am1911,1213.22)

Necklace
AD 900–1600
Lake Guatavita
Stone
L 122 cm, Diam. 3 cm
The British Museum
(Am1911,1213.27)

Tairona

The Tairona lived in the coastal bays running along the foot of the Sierra Nevada. They farmed and fished, and also mined salt. They produced realistic and fantastic human and animal-inspired ornaments. From around AD 900 they settled further up the mountains, building stone cities, such as Ciudad Perdida, and developing impressive agricultural terraces.

Pectoral
AD 200–900
Tairona (Nahuange)
Gold alloy
H 9.4 cm, W 21 cm
Museo del Oro (O16130)

Necklace with claws
and red beads
AD 900–1600
Tairona
Stone, gold alloy
L 58 cm
Museo del Oro
(O20294, L09942)

In ancient Colombia, men and
women decorated themselves
for ceremonies and rituals. They
painted their faces and bodies,
filed their teeth, bound their limbs,
and wore gold ornaments such as
headdresses, nose rings, earrings,
lip plugs and pendants.

Nose ornament
AD 900–1600
Tairona
Gold alloy
H 3.5 cm, W 6.5 cm
Museo del Oro (O14011)

Lip ornament
AD 900–1600
Tairona
Gold alloy
H 2.9 cm, L 4.6 cm
Museo del Oro (O16388)

Nose ornament
AD 900–1600
Tairona
Gold alloy
H 3 cm, W 7.4 cm
Museo del Oro (O26113)

Nose ornament
AD 900–1600
Tairona
Gold alloy
H 5.8, W 7.6 cm
Museo del Oro (O22822)

Zenú

The Zenú lived in the tropical
Caribbean plains, a region
of marshes, estuaries and
grasslands. They controlled the
water by building a system of
canals and artificial platforms.
At the height of their civilization,
they buried their leaders in tombs
with impressive gold breastplates
and other ornaments.

False filigree earrings
200 BC – AD 1000
Early Zenú
Gold alloy
Each H 5.2 W 8.8
Museo del Oro (O32413,
O32414)

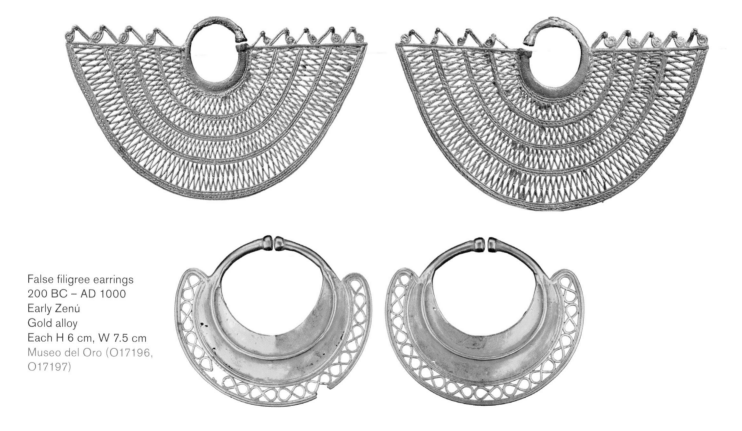

False filigree earrings
200 BC – AD 1000
Early Zenú
Gold alloy
Each H 6 cm, W 7.5 cm
Museo del Oro (O17196,
O17197)

Nose ornament
200 BC – AD 1000
Early Zenú
Gold alloy
H 4.5 cm, W 13.6 cm
Museo del Oro (O01409)

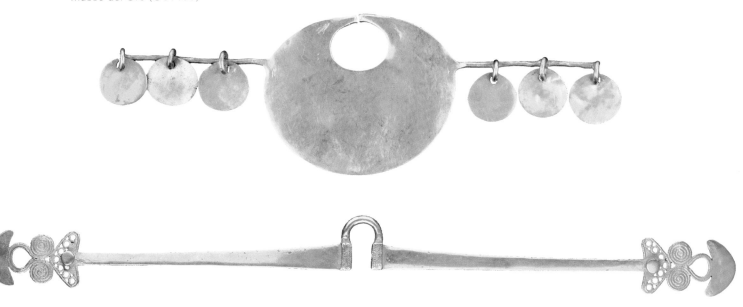

Nose ornament
Gold alloy
200 BC – AD 1000
Early Zenú
H 2.2 cm, W 29.1 cm
Museo del Oro (O31876)

Nose ornament
AD 600–1600
Muisca
Gold alloy
H 5 cm, W 17.7 cm
Museo del Oro (O06077)

Muisca

People in the Muisca region
settled on the high plains of
the Andes around AD 600.
Their homes were scattered
over the mountainsides
and valleys, but they came
together at important times
of the year for ceremonies in
which gold was particularly
important, for instance
those that took place at
Lake Guatavita.

Nose ornament with
hanging plates
AD 600–1600
Muisca
Gold alloy
H 7.7 cm, W 8.3 cm
Museo del Oro (O08306)

Tunjo (votive figure) with
nose ornament
AD 600–1600
Muisca
Gold alloy
H 12.2 cm, W 3 cm
Museo del Oro (O06361)

Quimbaya

The Quimbaya lived in
valleys in farming and
mining communities. Early
Quimbaya people cast very
fine objects such as the
mask pectoral (opposite)
in the shape of a face, with
filed teeth and wearing a
nose ornament. Later they
created mainly hammered
pieces. The Quimbaya
were one of the strongest
chiefdoms in fighting against
the Spanish invasion of
their territories.

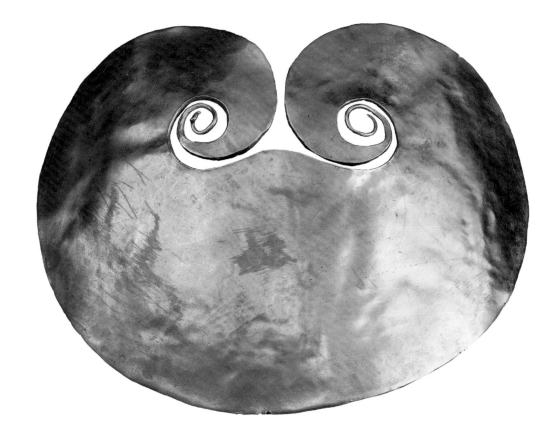

Pectoral
500 BC – AD 1600
Quimbaya
Gold alloy
H 16 cm, W 20 cm, D 3 cm
The British Museum
(Am1978,Q4)

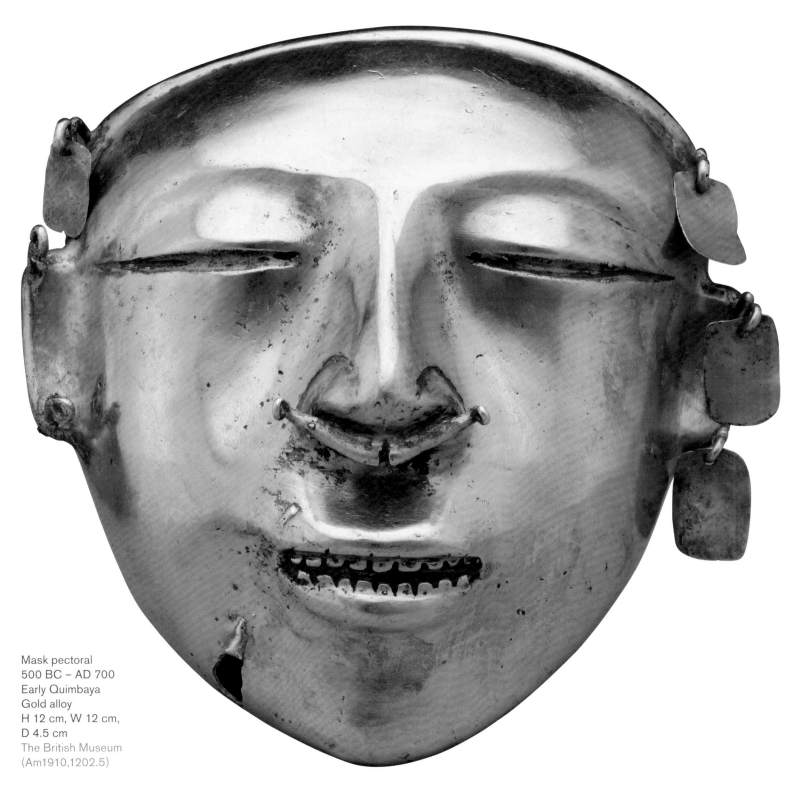

Mask pectoral
500 BC – AD 700
Early Quimbaya
Gold alloy
H 12 cm, W 12 cm,
D 4.5 cm
The British Museum
(Am1910,1202.5)

Tolima

The Tolima lived around Colombia's main river, the Magdalena. In the early first century they produced fine, abstract, symmetrical pieces from gold and other metals. By the time the Spanish arrived, the area was inhabited by groups of farmers and fishermen, and the metalwork was far simpler.

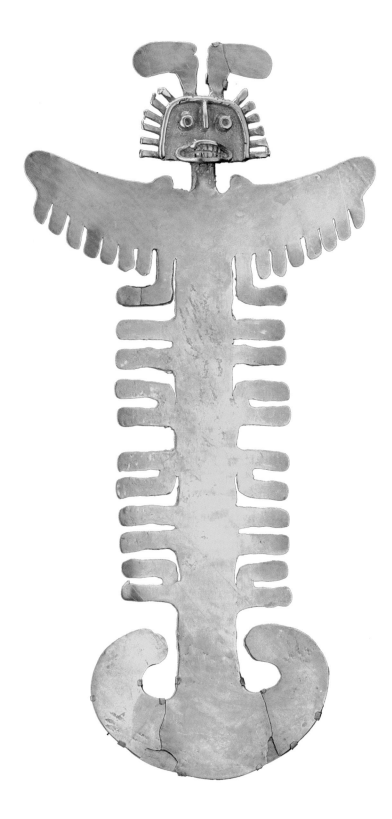

Pectoral
1 BC – AD 700
Early Tolima
Gold alloy
H 20.9 cm, W 10.6 cm
Museo del Oro (O06796)

Pectoral
1 BC – AD 700
Early Tolima
Gold alloy
H 32 cm, W 16.2 cm
Museo del Oro (O06061)

Calima-Malagana

The earliest evidence of farming communities in the Calima region dates from around 1500 BC. By AD 100 people were living in valleys, terracing hillsides and building irrigation for their crops. Metalworkers created impressive pectorals, diadems, nose rings and other decorative objects.

Nose ornament with hanging plates
200 BC – AD 1300
Calima-Malagana (Yotoco-Malagana)
Gold alloy
H 13 cm, W 5.7 cm
Museo del Oro (O04319)

Pectoral
200 BC – AD 1300
Calima-Malagana (Yotoco-
Malagana)
Gold alloy
H 22.5 cm, W 27.5 cm
Museo del Oro (O04832)

Calima goldsmiths were masters of the hammering technique. Some of the most elaborate objects they produced are decorated with fine repoussé images and patterns. In some exceptional examples, dangling plates and other ornaments are attached to the figures represented, as in this diadem where the central image wears large earspools and a nose ornament.

Diadem
200 BC – AD 1300
Calima-Malagana
(Yotoco-Malagana)
Gold alloy
H 27 cm, W 26 cm
Museo del Oro (O05202)

Ritual identity

The female figure opposite
shows how men and women
in ancient Colombia may
have painted their bodies.
The designs and colours
would have helped to
show a person's identity
and status in a community,
and been used to mark
important rites of passage
and transformation rituals.
The paints would have been
applied using small sticks
and brushes or with roller
stamps, such as these
ceramic ones, which allowed
complex and repeated
patterns to be printed
on the skin. Some have
dotted designs that might
recreate jaguar spots, while
geometric designs might
represent snakeskin.

Roller stamp for body
painting
AD 900–1600
Tairona
Ceramic
H 9.1 cm, Diam. 4.1 cm
Museo del Oro (C03124)

Roller stamp for body
painting
AD 900–1600
Tairona
Ceramic
H 8.2 cm, Diam. 4.4 cm
Museo del Oro (C10788)

Roller stamp for body
painting
200 BC – AD 1000
Early Zenú
Ceramic
H 6.1 cm, Diam. 7.5 cm
Museo del Oro (C05255)

Female figure
6000–2000 BC
Formative Zenú
Ceramic
H 19.5 cm, Diam. 13.7 cm
Museo del Oro (C13396)

Men and women also marked themselves using a wide range of permanent body decorations, including scarification and piercing. Scarification was a form of body decoration made by cutting the skin to form scar patterns from the healing wound. The figure opposite wears a twisted nose ring similar to the one illustrated alongside. People also pierced the upper part of their ear lobes and below the lips.

Mask with incisions
1600 BC – AD 100
Calima-Malagana (Ilama)
Ceramic
H 16.8 cm, Diam. 16.8 cm
Museo del Oro (C11199)

Nose ornament
AD 900–1600
Late Cauca
Gold alloy
H 2.5 cm, Diam. 2.5 cm
The British Museum
(Am+5804)

Figure with nose ornament
AD 900–1600
Late Cauca
Ceramic
H 23 cm, W 17.5 cm
Museo del Oro (C12697)

The power of gold

In ancient Colombia, gold was valued not only for its aesthetic properties, but also for its association with the sun.

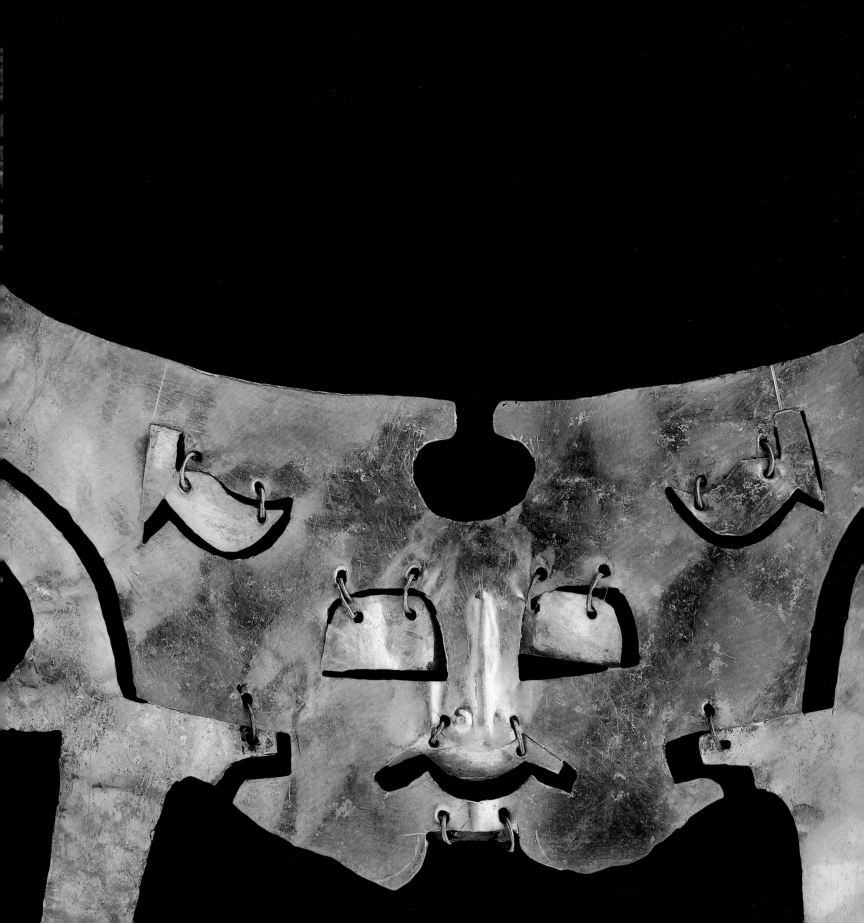

1   The power of gold

In ancient Colombia, gold was not desired for its economic value or used as currency, but instead had an important cultural, ritual and symbolic role. Gold was linked to the spiritual forces of creation and transformation; thus the materiality of metal objects was able to act as a bridge between the mental and physical worlds.

Gold's bright yellowish colour and reflective properties, together with its incorruptible nature and durability, imbued it with a special power and conjured associations with the sun. Gold objects would have shined and reflected the sun's rays, giving the wearer a direct connection with this divine star. Venerated by many pre-Hispanic cultures, the sun was full of energy and creative forces, while also being strongly associated with male activities. Gold was the perfect metaphor for the sun's regenerative power and could act as a mediator between humans and the supernatural world.

In contrast, metals that decayed easily and had a tendency to change colour and alter their appearance were strongly associated with the moon, which, unlike the sun, followed a cycle marking its death and rebirth in the night sky. In the Andean view of the cosmos both silver and copper were related to the moon: their colours bore a similarity to it and both metals were associated with women and female fertility.[1] Silver and platinum were worked to a smaller degree in south-west Colombia and were always alloyed with other metals.

Yet in pre-Hispanic Colombia gold and the naturally occurring silver in alluvial gold were usually combined with copper to create the alloy known as *tumbaga*. With this amalgamation of metals, the artisan was able to achieve a lower melting point – from about 1,064°C for pure gold to around 910°C for gold-copper alloy and even lower if silver was present (767°C) – which made it easier to work and allowed for finer details in the casting process. At the same time *tumbaga* was harder than pure gold, which allowed for sturdier pieces and for the construction of small tools. *Tumbaga* was not only valued for its strength, but also because the possibility of manipulating the proportions of the basic elements of gold, silver and copper meant that differences in colour, and even the smell and taste of the resulting alloy, could induce different sensory perceptions.

From the mining of the metal to the acquisition of a finished piece, gold followed complex trade routes and changed hands several times. Gold mining

1. Falchetti 2003, p. 347.

Indians panning gold in the early Colonial period. Woodcut from *La Historia General y Natural de las Indias*, Gonzalo Fernández de Oviedo y Valdés, 1535–58.

was a seasonal occupation in some production areas, determined by the dry and low season that changed the flow of rivers and facilitated the panning of gold nuggets. In the principal gold-sourcing areas, such as the northern mountains of Antioquia where the important mining site of Buriticá was situated (see map p. 11), full-time workers would have invested their efforts year-round in sourcing this precious metal from alluvial rivers and the veins of the earth. From the mining sources, gold would have been traded along different routes to the principal craft production centres, such as the major metalworking site of Dabeiba. There metals and alloys were smelted in crucibles, ceramic ovens and furnaces, where the desired temperature was reached by the blowing of air into the fire with blowpipes. The result was a small round piece of metal, known as a *tejuelo* or ingot, formed at the bottom of the crucible (see p. 62). In Dabeiba and other metalworking sites goldsmiths produced fine finished pieces and *tejuelos* that were then traded further afield to local communities and distant chiefdoms to be reworked by local artists.

In pre-Hispanic Colombia two processes, hammering and casting, were employed for the crafting of metal objects. Hammering predominated in the south-west of Colombia, as in Calima territory. Cylindrical stone anvils with small oval hammers were used for the hammering; handling these required expert knowledge of the technique. After repeated hammering of the *tejuelos*, the metal sheet would become brittle. Before it cracked or broke it was reheated

53

'How the Guianians are Accustomed to cast their gold images.' Engraving by Theodor de Bry from his *Grand Voyages*, 1599. This is an imaginative recreation of a gold-casting process by Theodor de Bry, who never visited America. Casting of objects with two-part solid moulds in ancient Colombia can only be attested by one exceptional *brasero* (incense burner), from the famous Treasure of the Quimbaya, now in the Museo de América, Madrid.

and then cooled down by being dipped in water to allow further hammering and shaping (a technique known as annealing). The process would be repeated several times until the required shape and thickness of metal was achieved.

One of the decorating methods used on hammered metal was repoussé. A design would be drawn on the surface of the metal sheet and, with the help of tools made of *tumbaga*, stone or horn, the design would be imprinted by pressing on the metal sheet with a soft piece of leather or a bag of sand placed underneath the gold. The metal would be gradually worked from both sides until the design was completed.

Once finished, metal pieces could be joined by various methods, including pinning with gold clips, staples or laces, bending the edges to clinch sheets, hammer-welding and soldering. More complex techniques known as granulation or diffusion bonding were also employed, in which a copper compound was mixed with an organic adhesive, then used to stick gold elements into place. The glue was burnt away in a heating process, leaving a barely perceptible join.

Colombian artists excelled at the casting of both large and small objects. Casting techniques became particularly elaborate in the central and northern areas of Colombia, for example in the Early Quimbaya and Muisca regions. Most of the cast pieces, either solid or hollow with openwork, were skilfully produced by the technique known as the lost-wax method. Beeswax from stingless bees (*Tetragonisca angustula*) was used to create the required shapes that incorporated lacing elements, coils and intricate details. Channels and pouring orifices to allow the molten gold to circulate were also produced in beeswax and attached to the pieces. The wax was fully enveloped with several layers of fine clay and once the mould was finished it was fired. The wax was then melted and poured out to leave space for the molten gold that would be poured in to cast the final piece. After cooling the metal, the clay mould was broken and the object extracted and finished by cutting off the excess pieces and pouring channels. This technique created unique pieces, as each time the mould was destroyed in the process and a new wax figure had to be produced to create the next object. Goldsmiths therefore not only had to be skilled at metalworking, but also at sculpting in wax and clay.[2] They required a precise knowledge and control of firing temperatures to achieve successful results. Exceptionally in Muisca territory stone matrices, carved on six sides with several small decorative elements, were used to mass-produce wax moulds for casting necklace beads and ornaments.[3] Among all the metalworking achievements in pre-Hispanic Colombia it was the double-mould hollow-casting technique that produced the most technologically complex and stunning objects. The manufacturing of hollow objects required a double mould, one for the interior core and one for the external shape. A core mould made of clay and charcoal was produced and dried completely before being covered with a coat of fine beeswax in the desired shape. The pouring channels and air vents were also added in wax. To secure it into position several supports made of wood were incised a centimetre deep through the wax and the inner mould. The whole piece was then covered in another layer of porous clay to create the external mould, then the wax was melted and the molten gold poured in. Once it had cooled the external mould was broken to free the piece, and through the open channels left by the wooden pegs or the natural openings of the shape the internal mould was broken and taken away. The small circular holes left by the wooden pegs were filled with metal.

The pieces were then finished by several gilding and burnishing techniques. Of these, depletion gilding was most commonly used in *tumbaga* pieces, which consisted of heating up the object in an oxidizing atmosphere, causing the oxidization of the copper. The item was then dipped in a liquid made from the

2. Muisca votive objects are frequently left unpolished, with traces of the channels that helped to create them left apparent. This remaining evidence of the original wax model is testament to its importance in the process.

3. The shapes were imprinted in soft clay. Once dry, the moulds were covered with a thin layer of beeswax, and the shape in the matrix was imprinted again in the interior of the wax shape. The result was a small wax shape that could be easily produced and repeated to cast objects.

55

An imaginative depiction of a method of melting and hammering gold alloy and other objects. From *History of the New World* by Girolamo Benzoni, originally published in Venice in 1565.

juice of plants, mixed with water and salt; this created an acid reaction which removed the base metal on the surface. The superficial layer that remained was rich in gold, while the core of the piece concealed the *tumbaga* alloy. This, together with other techniques such as *raspado zonificado* (zoned scraping) of oxide surface layers, enabled craftsmen to produce contrasting designs with a copper and gold finish. Goldsmiths also produced pieces combining several alloys, thus creating colour differences within single objects.

Ancient Colombian artists were able to produce spectacular objects using a combination of several techniques, including casting, hammering, treatment of the surfaces and the joining of pieces. The works are remarkable both in terms of their size, complexity and fine detailing, as well as in their imaginative compositions and the unique artistic rendering. The people who produced those objects were held in particularly high esteem. In some cases, such as in the Guatavita region, goldsmiths were itinerant from one community to another; while they were away, their services to the Guatavita lord had to be carried out by the temporary exchange of two vassals, denoting their importance and value.[4]

Chronicles, such as the Lenguazaque document, report how goldsmiths, who passed their skills from father to son, specialized in crafting objects either for body adornment or for votive and ritual use to be sacrificed to the gods. This is an important division that highlights the different uses of *tumbaga* objects in pre-Hispanic Colombia and how they were symbolically charged depending on the final shape and function given to the piece. Not only was gold a material associated with the sun, but a final object produced in gold alloys by specialized hands was infused with social meaning and imbued with divine power.

Ancient Colombian artists worked metals in a variety of styles and techniques, the best examples probably commissioned, owned and used by the highest elites. Those pieces show a level of refinement, both in the most naturalistic examples as well as in the more fantastic and imaginative shapes, that still fascinates us today.

4. Castellanos 1589

Three jaguars

Gold was not often used
alone, but was usually
melted with copper to create
an alloy known as *tumbaga*.
These jaguar ornaments
show how goldsmiths varied
the amounts of copper and
gold, which included
naturally occurring silver,
to produce colour ranging
from reddish to yellow. The
blend could also change
the smell, taste and shine
of the gold.

Tumbaga is a stronger metal
than pure gold, and has a
lower melting point, making
it easier to cast. Goldsmiths
blended different quantities
of metals depending on local
resources, or on the effect
they wished to achieve.

Feline-shaped pendants
AD 300–1600, 200 BC –
AD 1000, AD 300–1600
Early Zenú, Urabá, Urabá
Gold alloy
H 4.7 cm, W 2.8 cm
H 6.2 cm, W 3.3 cm
H 3.9 cm, W 2.2 cm
Museo del Oro (O32481,
O17255, O33611)

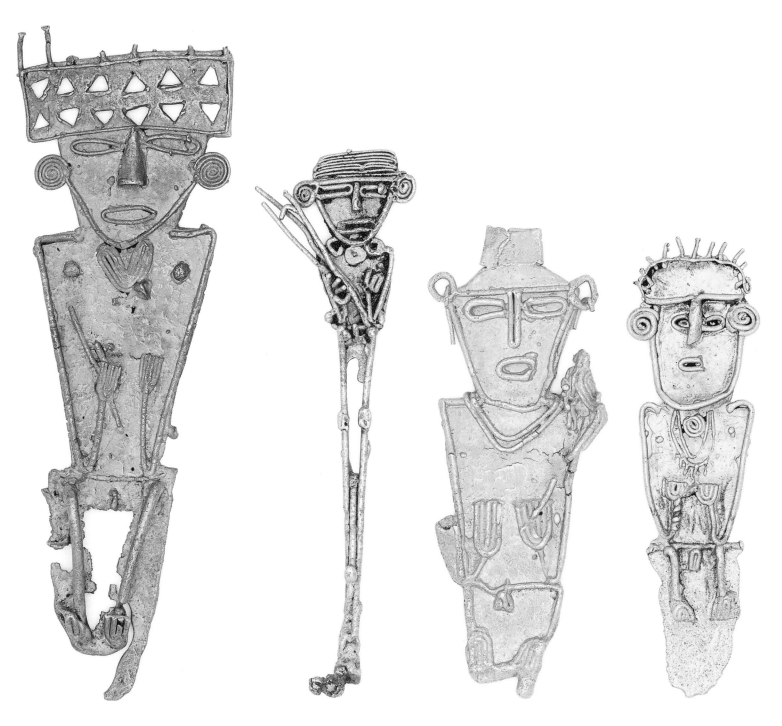

Group of *tunjos*
(votive figures)
AD 600–1600
Muisca
Gold alloy
H 4–9 cm, W 1.5–3.5 cm
The British Museum
(Am7460, Am1949,14.1,
Am1922,1116.1, AmS1321,
Am1847,0323.2,
Am1847,0323.3
Am1959,03.1, Am1895,17,
Am1949,07.2)

Tunjos

Tunjos, or votive offerings, were placed by Muisca people across their territory, under special landmarks such as rocks and trees, and in caves, rivers and lakes – places believed to be gateways to different worlds. *Tunjos* usually depict male and female figures, animals, as well as groups and scenes, all providing a window into Muisca life and rituals. Muisca artisans left the figures unpolished, and did not mend mistakes made in the casting process. These were not objects of beauty to be admired, but their imagery and the metal itself were important in communicating with the supernatural.

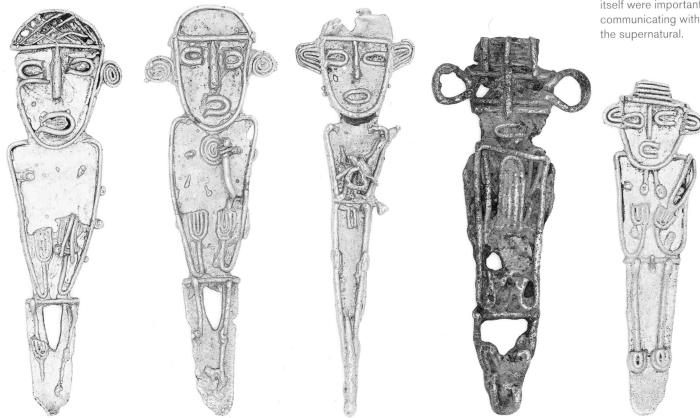

Metal-working tools

Goldsmiths melted small pebbles of metal and hammered them on stone anvils, or used them for casting. They had stone and metal chisels of different sizes for cutting and shaping sheets of gold alloy. Small, portable tools such as these were precious belongings owned by highly regarded and specialized artisans who may have travelled between goldworking centres.

Metal-working tools
AD 600–1600
Late Nariño, Tairona, Muisca
Stone, gold alloy
Each H 1.7 cm, H 1.6 cm,
H 4.2 cm, H 5.5 cm, H 7.7
cm, H 7.9 cm, H 5 cm
Museo del Oro (L00299,
L00757, O31995, L02682,
L02724)

Cylindrical bracelets
AD 900–1600
Tairona
Gold alloy
Each H 4.3 cm, Diam. 6.3 cm
Museo del Oro (O16156,7)

Hammered gold sheets could be shaped into a variety of objects including body ornaments, such as the cylindrical bracelets opposite. Sometimes sheets were assembled to form larger, more complex pieces. Here sheets of gold have been joined with small loops to create an articulated nose ornament, which would have partially covered the face and jingled and moved with its wearer.

Nose ornament
200 BC – AD 1300
Calima-Malagana
(Yotoco-Malagana)
Gold alloy
H 10 cm, W 15 cm
The British Museum
(Am+5802)

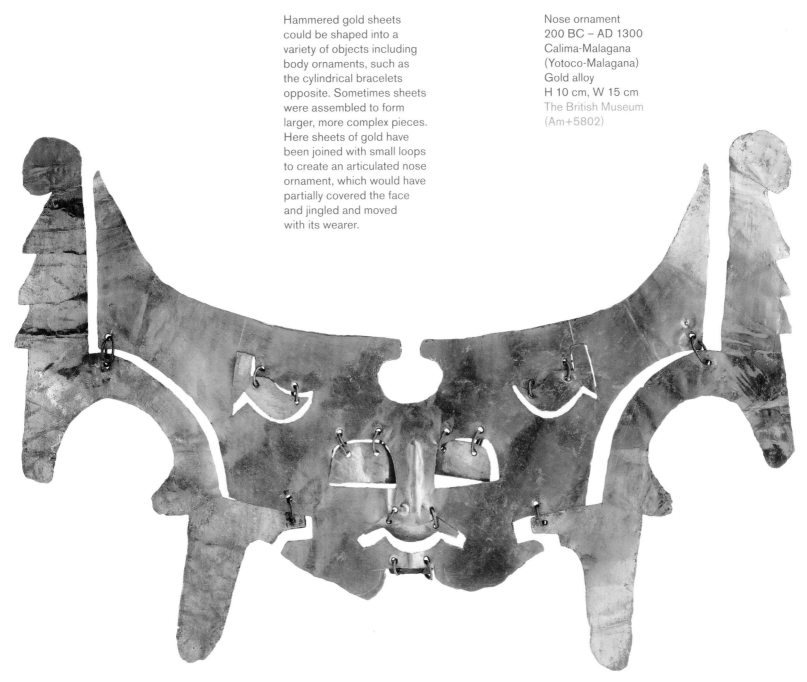

These beads were
hammered and crafted into
insects. Each piece was
folded into shape and later
strung together. The many
small pieces were combined
with stone beads to create a
spectacular necklace.

Necklace
1600 BC – AD 100
Calima-Malagana (Ilama)
Gold alloy
Each bead H 5.5 cm
Museo del Oro (O06519 &
L03332)

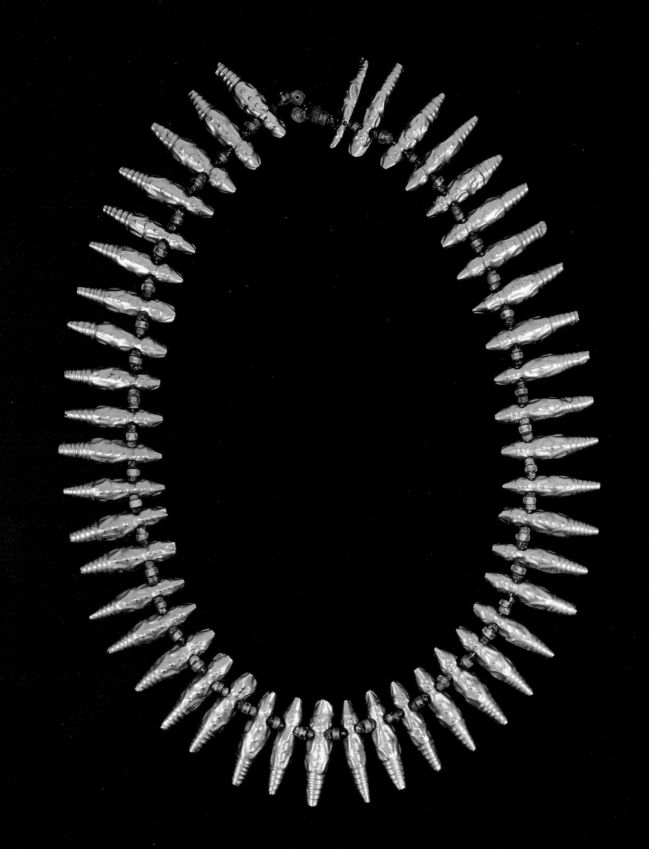

Once gold had been hammered it could be worked and decorated in different ways. This earring pendant shows a feline face, made using the repoussé technique, creating a high-relief decorative image. The jaguar flask (opposite) is a unique masterpiece. The maker has folded very thin sheets of gold to create a three-dimensional shape, and then clipped it and added other features, such as impressive claws and a tail. The jaguar's nose ring is made of platinum, a rare and highly valued metal in ancient Colombia.

Earring pendant
AD 600–1600
Late Nariño
Gold alloy
Diam. 9.9 cm
Museo del Oro (O25397)

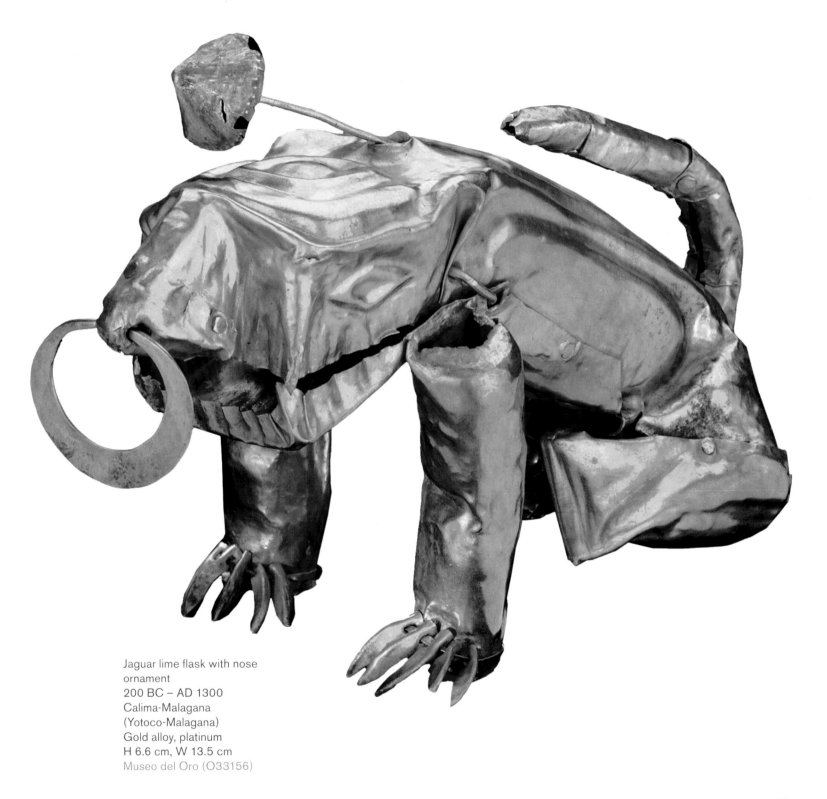

Jaguar lime flask with nose
ornament
200 BC – AD 1300
Calima-Malagana
(Yotoco-Malagana)
Gold alloy, platinum
H 6.6 cm, W 13.5 cm
Museo del Oro (O33156)

Lost-wax casting

Lost-wax casting was a common technique used by goldsmiths to make intricate objects, such as the end of this lime dipper (opposite). Goldsmiths first modelled the shape of the object in beeswax with intricate detail, and added pouring channels. They covered this in thin layers of clay to make a mould (right). Once the clay was baked, they removed the liquid wax and poured molten gold into the space. When the mould had cooled they broke away the clay, revealing the original design, now in gold *tumbaga*. Finally they broke off the extra pieces of metal left by the pouring channels and polished the surface. Ceramic moulds were made to be broken as part of the casting process, to free the final metal object. This is a rare example that has survived. Additional elements could be added to the final piece, such as the dangling round earspools worn by the figure on the lime dipper (opposite).

Mould
200 BC – AD 1300
Calima-Malagana
(Yotoco-Malagana)
Ceramic
H 6 cm, Diam. 4.4 cm
Museo del Oro (C13452)

Lime dipper with
anthropomorphic finial and
hanging earspools
200 BC – AD 1300
Calima-Malagana
(Yotoco-Malagana)
Gold alloy
H 31.5 cm, W 1.6 cm
Museo del Oro (O05234)

Matrix casting

Carved stone matrices were used primarily by Muisca goldsmiths. Every inch of the surface was crowded with imagery to make the most of this tool. The same matrix could be used several times to mass produce sets of similar pieces for larger ornaments. More robust objects, such as the figure opposite, were also created using individual hand-made wax figures and the lost-wax casting technique.

Matrix
AD 600–1600
Muisca
Stone
H 11.5 cm, W 6 cm, D 3 cm
The British Museum
(Am1925,1211.1)

Necklace beads
AD 600–1600
Muisca
Gold alloy
Each H 2.5 cm
The British Museum
(Am1937,0706,11)

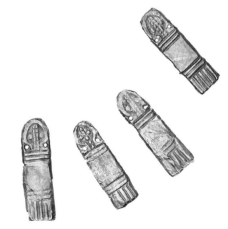

Anthropomorphic pendant
500 BC – AD 700
Early Quimbaya
Gold alloy
H 6.5 cm, W 5.8 cm
Museo del Oro (O03065)

Double-mould casting

Quimbaya goldsmiths used
the lost-wax technique with
double-moulds (see p. 55) to
produce spectacular hollow
objects, such as these lime
flasks (*poporo*). They are some
of the most technically complex
and stunning objects found
in the Americas. The design
and material of lime containers
(used in ritual coca-chewing,
see pp. 130–40) varied
according to the owner's
status and the wealth of the
community. The two figures
here are represented fully
naked, with body ornaments,
including piercings, and
marks on their legs to indicate
body binding. They hold ritual
implements or plants in their
hands. On the male figure's
left side a mistake made during
casting has been mended,
showing that this was a valued
object. The female figure is
seated on a stool, a sign of
high rank and status.

Standing male *poporo* (lime
container)
500 BC – AD 700
Early Quimbaya
Gold alloy
H 30 cm, W 15 cm, D 6 cm
The British Museum
(Am1889,1001.1)

Seated female *poporo* (lime
container)
500 BC – AD 700
Early Quimbaya
Gold alloy
H 14.5 cm, W 7.5 cm, D 5.5 cm
The British Museum
(Am1940,11.2)

75

Disc
AD 600–1600
Late Nariño
Gold alloy
Diam. 14.9 cm
Museo del Oro (O21220)

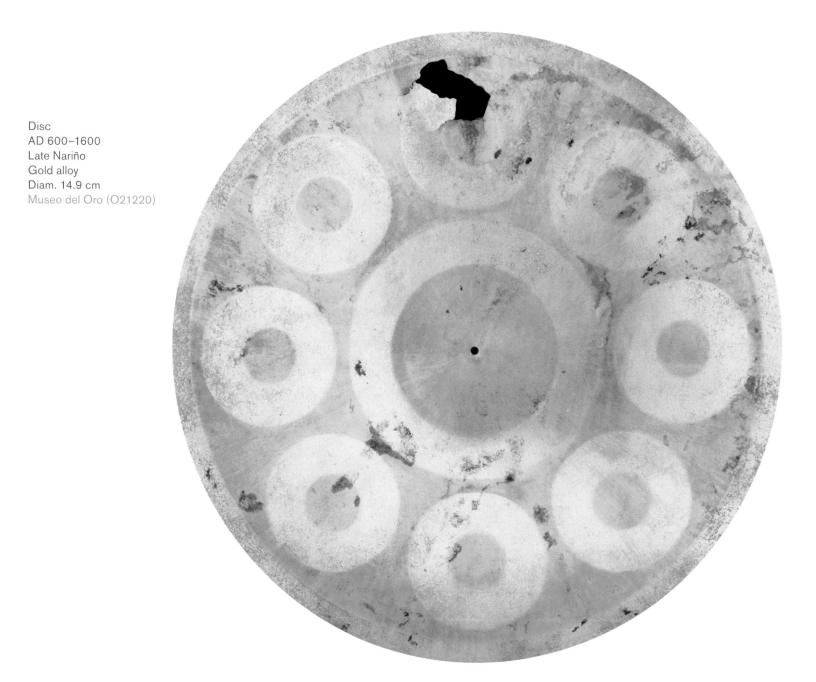

Lime dipper with
anthropomorphic finial
200 BC – AD 1300
Calima-Malagana
(Yotoco-Malagana)
Gold alloy
H 22.6 cm, W 2.1 cm
Museo del Oro (O06432)

Colour effects

The final stage in the
working of a cast or
hammered object was the
treatment of its surface.
The disc (opposite) shows
how gold alloy could be
treated to create different
colour effects. The piece
would have been treated
with depletion gilding before
selectively removing some
of the gilding to expose the
colour of the base alloy and
create contrasting designs.
It was probably designed
to rotate, suspended from
a string though its central
hole, to produce light and
movement effects, possibly
at religious ceremonies.

This dipper (left) was
cast in two stages. First
the goldsmith cast the
headdress and the objects
the figure is holding in one
alloy. This was then recast
with the rest of the figure
and the long stem in a
different alloy combination,
creating a colour effect.

Seashell-shaped pendant
AD 900–1600
Tairona
Gold alloy
H 20.4 cm, W 4.9 cm
Museo del Oro (O21215)

This piece has been treated
by the depletion-gilding
technique. After heating
the object, causing the
oxidation of the copper, it
was dipped in a liquid made
from the juices of plants,
mixed with water and salt.
This created an acid reaction
that removed the copper at
the surface and left a layer of
gold visible.

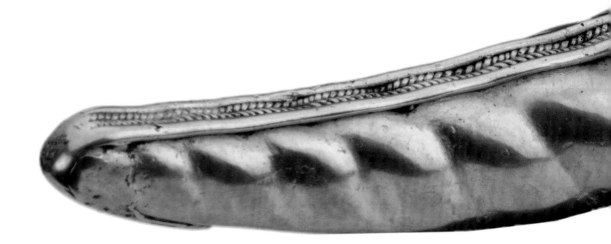

More than gold

Gold had a special symbolic status for the people of ancient Colombia, but it was just one of the many materials they valued.

More than gold

From the earliest times, visitors to Colombia focused their attention on the ancient gold objects produced there. But this fixation did little justice to the wide range of objects made in – and often highly valued by – pre-Hispanic societies. In many cases such objects, made of perishable materials, have not survived, but where they have they can enhance our understanding of pre-Columbian communities. They include stone tools used to work gold, such as anvils, goldworkers' moulds, carved stone matrices, and polishing tools and chisels used for embossing and treating gold surfaces. Alongside gold ornaments, other kinds of body decorations have also survived, such as pendants and necklaces made of colourful stone beads.

The most notable surviving objects, however, are ceramics, which were skilfully crafted by specialists using time-consuming techniques; they are remarkable for their exquisite finishes, creative shapes and diversity of styles. Research into such pieces has furthered our understanding of pre-Hispanic communities and their belief systems: we have gained information about the manufacture and use of the ceramics themselves, while the painted and modelled decorations on them has furthered our knowledge of pre-Hispanic society. Body-painting tools, such as ceramic stamps (see pp. 47, 96, 113), have also survived. Cylindrical stamps display continuous bas-relief designs across their surface, which were rolled across the skin to leave a repeating design; some ceramics actually depict people with painted or stamped designs on their skin (see p. 47). Such body decorations had a ritual transformative purpose. Animal pelts, bird feathers, body paint and elaborate regalia were seen as a second skin which could define and transform the person wearing them.

Gold itself did not always survive. The insatiable thirst for gold that led Europeans to the conquest of the New World was reflected in the colonial laws that were passed to control the looting and systematic plundering of indigenous settlements. Handcrafted objects were categorized as 'idols' in early colonial documents and their seizure was directed by royal mandate: religion was used to justify their destruction for the greater good of the people. In 1550 a ruling of the Real Audiencia de Santa Fe[1] dictated that all objects manufactured by indigenous people be divided into two categories. Objects made of gold and emerald were collected, and the gold was melted down in the furnaces of currency houses. Objects made from feathers, wood, shell and bone were

1. The Real Audiencia de Santa Fe, created in 1549, was the highest court of the Spanish Crown in the territory of the New Kingdom of Granada.

2. Nuñez de Balboa 1829

3. After Bray 1979, p. 143

Frog-shaped bead
AD 900–1600
Tairona
Stone
H 3.5 cm, W 3 cm
Museo del Oro (L02233)

Zoomorphic bead
AD 900–1600
Tairona
Stone
H 2.5 cm, W 1.5 cm
Museo del Oro (L02303)

considered 'idols of the devil', and were systematically confiscated from their owners and destroyed. Some of these, however, escaped this methodical destruction and have survived in museum collections.

Colonial chronicles make passing descriptions that give us an insight into the valuable materials traded and used in ancient Colombia. Vasco Núñez de Balboa reported in 1513 how the cacique Dabeiba made payments with 'peccaries, of which there are many in this land, and much fish, cotton cloth and salt, and also such objects of worked gold as they desire'.[2] Foodstuffs, including plants, fish and animals, appear to have been traded across the diverse Colombian landscape, from high-altitude communities to coastal groups and vice versa. The importance of some of these agricultural resources can be seen in the naturalistic and faithful representation of fruits and plants on exquisitely hand-crafted ceramics. Some ceramics also depict people fishing with nets. These, together with gold fish hooks, give some insight into fishing practices. Lake and river fish were probably traded across the landscape, while the two coastal regions – the Caribbean and Pacific – provided an array of diverse sea products valued in highland communities.

Seashells were a particularly important commodity across the Andes. Coastal shells used to make lime to chew with coca leaves were traded far inland, while conch-shell trumpets and shell ornaments have been found on archaeological sites in highland communities, for example in Muisca territory. Pedro Simón reported in 1625 that shells were traded from the Caribbean coast, passing from hand to hand at very high prices. Representations of shells in other materials, for example in stone and gold (see pp. 78 and 93), reflect their importance.

Textiles were also widely traded. Clothing marked social status and identity in ancient America, and ancient Colombian textile production is documented in colonial sources. Father Zamora noted that 'the women are continually spinning yarn for the mantles which they wear, and for those of their sons and husbands'.[3] Women seem to have carried out the tasks of spinning, weaving, and probably decorating textiles for daily use and ritual practices. They produced complex woven textiles, made of cotton or camelid fibre (such as alpaca wool). Some textiles were painted with decorative designs, while others had colourful feathers and other objects sewn onto them, for example metal discs that must have dangled and shimmered as the wearer moved.

Very few textiles have survived from ancient Colombia, but some exceptional examples from Muisca territory have reached museum collections thanks to their preservation as part of funerary bundles. A Muisca cotton textile (see p. 98), woven with paired warps and a vertical stripe in supplementary warp in

Parts of certain animals, such as jaguar skin, tails and claws, were highly valued in ancient Colombian societies, used for ritual and worn at ceremonies. Although they haven't survived, real claws were probably used to create necklace designs such as this gold one.

Necklace with claw-shaped beads
200 BC – AD 1000
Early Zenú
Gold alloy
Diam. 58 cm
Museo del Oro (O06537, O33581)

brown along each side, is a rare surviving fragment of a decorated textile. It is painted with images of squatting figures and the type of geometric designs that also occur on Muisca pottery. In 1625 Pedro Simón described some Muisca textiles that he encountered at La Tora (on the River Magdalena) 'of very fine cotton, well woven, and painted by means of brushes (in the fashion of the Indians of this Kingdom), with narrow coloured bands, which they call *maures*, running the length of the cloth, and with other little designs'. He also commented on the fact that textiles were sold at fixed prices, corroborating what Vasco Núñez de Balboa reported about materials exchanged with the cacique Dabeiba in Zenú territory.

It seems that across ancient Colombia materials of different types were connected by certain sensory elements, such as their iridescence or brilliance. The glistening of gold was especially important, but in his description of the rituals at Lake Guatavita (see Introduction, p. 24) Juan Rodríguez Freyle makes clear that a variety of sensory elements played a crucial role in the occasion. The combination of vibrant colours, smells, movement and sounds transformed the everyday into an intense experience. Stone and gold bells, flutes, ocarinas and rattles all survive, attesting to the variety of sounds that accompanied these occasions.

Exotic feathers also played an important role in clothing and adornment; the brightest and most colourful ones were probably traded from the Amazonian lowlands. The iridescence of some feathers might have asserted their properties as mediators with the supernatural, and retained some of the powerful qualities of the birds from which they were taken. Very few feather objects dating back to pre-conquest times have survived, but some gold items represent people wearing feathers – for example as spectacular head ornaments (see p. 15). They are also briefly mentioned in chronicles as part of elaborate regalia. Juan Rodríguez Freyle, for example, wrote in 1636 that the raft sailing to the centre of Lake Guatavita was 'all loaded with an infinity of men and women dressed in fine plumes, golden plaques and crowns'. Other accounts describe chiefs wearing not only featherwork, but also other kinds of headdresses, animal skins and body painting: 'One of their leaders came to him wearing a carefully woven straw crown, all covered in feathers, and with his hair gathered up on his head and an otter skin hanging from his neck and slung over his shoulder, and his whole body painted with annatto; he looked like a monster.'[4]

The variety of these objects conveys a tangible sense of the richness of pre-Hispanic Colombian society; they must undoubtedly have animated occasions with a spectacular combination of glistening light, vibrant colours, movement and sounds.

This small rattle shows a person's face with a headdress made up of two feathered bird's heads. Such objects provide evidence for how such elaborate headdresses were worn by people in ancient Colombia.

Rattle
200 BC – AD 1000
Early Zenú
Gold alloy
H 5.6 cm, W 9 cm
Museo del Oro (O33753)

4. *Account of the Discovery of the Provinces of Antioquia by Jorge Robledo*, Juan Bautista Sardella, 1541.

Necklace
AD 900–1600
Tairona
Stone
L 27.5 cm
Museo del Oro (L03355)

Stone necklaces

Carved and polished stones
were traded across South
and Central America and
were used as offerings and
to make jewellery. Their
qualities, such as colour
or translucence, would
have given them different
symbolic meanings.

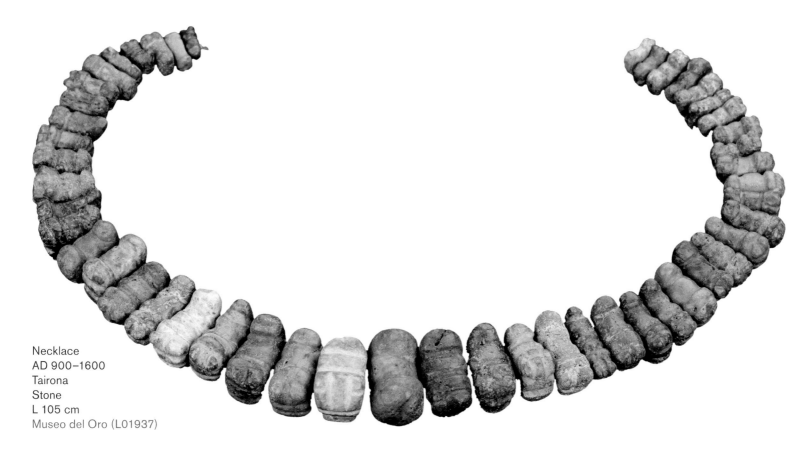

Necklace
AD 900–1600
Tairona
Stone
L 105 cm
Museo del Oro (L01937)

Necklace
200 BC – AD 1300
Calima-Malagana
(Yotoco-Malagana)
Stone
Each bead Diam. 3.2 cm
Museo del Oro (L00871)

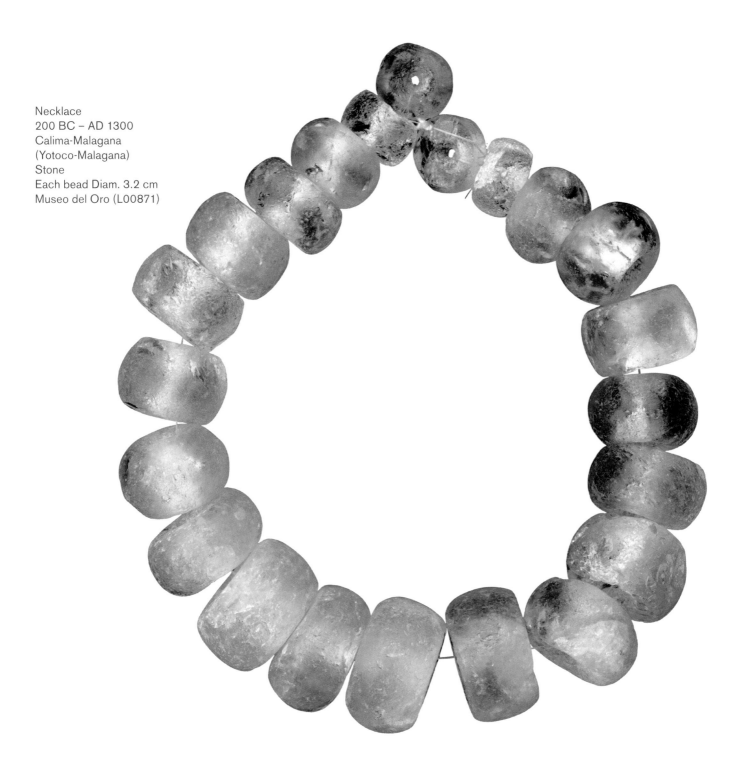

Basket-weaving

Basket-weaving would have been an important skill in ancient Colombia. Figures painted on ceramic and in gold are sometimes shown with basket-shaped bodies, suggesting that baskets were not just practical objects but had a wider symbolic significance.

Basket-bearer vessel
1600 BC – AD 100
Calima-Malagana (Ilama)
Ceramic
H 12.8 cm, Diam. 7 cm
Museo del Oro (C06304)

Flowers and plants

Many natural objects were copied in gold and also ceramic, suggesting that they were important in ritual as well as daily life. The beauty, colour, smell and healing properties of plants might have given them a special role in body adornment and ritual practice.

Pair of earrings
200 BC – AD 1300
Calima-Malagana
(Yotoco-Malagana)
Gold alloy
Each H 2 cm, Diam. 6 cm
Museo del Oro (O33391,
O33392)

Gourd-shaped vessel
500 BC – AD 700
Early Quimbaya
Ceramic
H 20.5 cm, Diam. 40 cm
Museo del Oro (C13360)

Shells

Seashells and land snail shells were highly valued throughout South and Central America. Traders carried a wide range from the Caribbean and Pacific coasts to highland communities. Conch shells were used for body ornaments and musical instruments, while some shells were crushed and ingested as part of ritual practices, and others were offered to the gods. The fact that shells were also cast in gold shows their importance and value to the ancient Colombian people.

Spondylus shell
AD 100–800
Shell
H 11 cm, W 11.5 cm, D 6 cm
The British Museum
(Am7437)

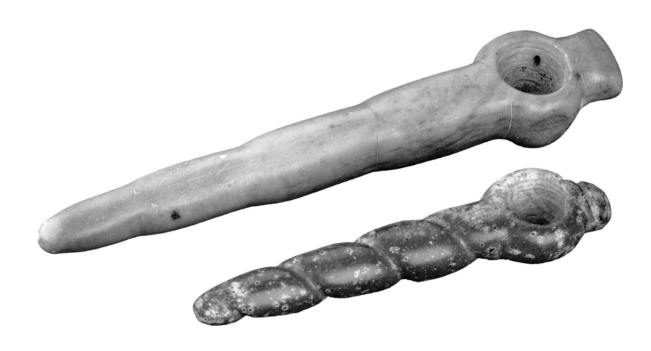

Seashell-shaped pendant
500 BC – AD 700
Early Quimbaya
Gold alloy
H 8 cm, W 2.5 cm, D 2 cm
The British Museum
(Am1910,1202.11)

Seashell-shaped pendant
AD 900–1600
Tairona
Stone
L 12.4 cm, W 1.9 cm, D 2.9 cm
Museo del Oro (L01566)

Seashell-shaped pendant
AD 900–1600
Tairona
Stone
H 18 cm, W 2.3 cm, D 3.2 cm
Museo del Oro (L01596)

Fishing and hunting

Finding food was essential for a community's survival. Activities such as hunting, fishing and sowing were all regulated and accompanied by ritual to ensure their success and to guarantee harmony in nature. These fish hooks made from gold may have been used in rituals related to fishing. The bowl shows men with antlers hunting deer with nets. Only members of the elite were allowed to hunt and eat deer. Furthermore, the imagery of half-man, half-deer figures suggests that deer held ritual significance for the community.

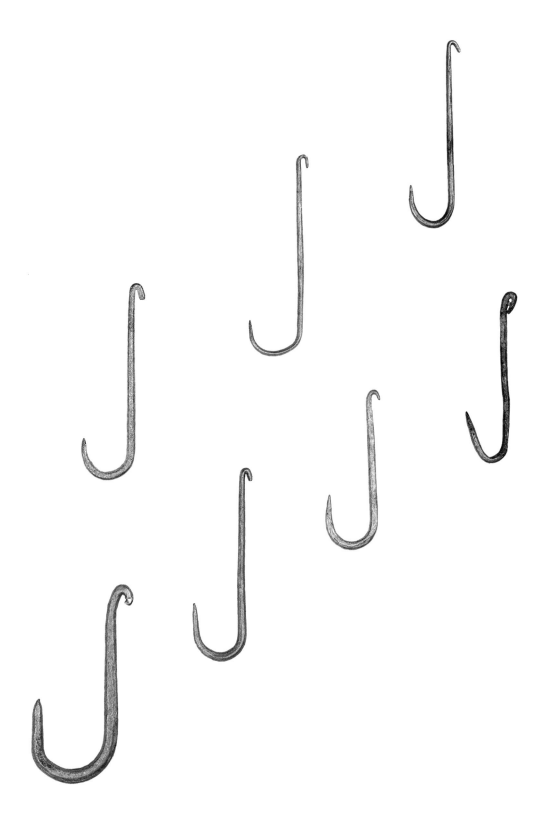

Fish hooks
AD 900–1600
Late Cauca
Gold alloy
Each H 3 cm, W 1 cm
The British Museum
(Am1958,03.33a&b, 35,
44a&b, 46, 58)

Painted dish
AD 600–1600
Late Nariño
Ceramic
H 8.6 cm, Diam. 11 cm
Museo del Oro (C05666)

Textiles

In most ancient American communities, women traditionally carried out tasks such as spinning, weaving and decorating cloth. Textiles were used for clothing, for exchange and payments of tribute to rulers, as well as for burying the dead. Different types of cloth might have defined men and women, as well as groups within a community. Painted and woven patterns were probably symbolic and would have conveyed important messages. Light to carry and versatile, cloth was the perfect way to express identity.

Spindle whorls were personal, portable decorated objects used for spinning and twisting fibres into yarn. In ancient Colombia, women would have used cotton and other vegetable fibres, as well as the hair of animals such as llamas and alpacas.

Seated female figure
AD 600–1600
Late Nariño
Ceramic
H 21.4 cm, Diam. 12.7 cm
Museo del Oro (C03099)

Spindle whorls
AD 600–1600
Muisca
Stone
Diam. 3–4.5 cm
Museo del Oro (L00382,
L01195, L00211, L01200,
L00321)

Few textiles have survived from ancient Colombia. This rare cloth has woven borders, with painted decorations in the centre. The design includes squatting figures, with bent legs and elbows resting on their knees. Their skull-like faces have hollowed cheeks and wide eyes, each surrounded by a large feathered headdress. The cloth was originally used for burial and the squatting pose of the figures may reflect the position of the body when it was wrapped. The spiral and interlocking patterns are typical of Muisca designs, and craftspeople used similar decoration on ceramic vessels and stone objects.

Painted textile
AD 1300–1400
Muisca
Cotton
L 135 cm, W 122 cm
The British Museum
(Am1842,1112.3)

Feathers

Feathers, with their bright iridescent colours, would have played an important role in ancient Colombian societies. European chronicles describe how they were woven, sometimes combined with basketry, and worn by high-status rulers and spiritual leaders. They are reminders of the rich array of materials and craftsmanship that has been lost with time.

Feather headdresses
20th century
Huitoto
Feather, fibre
Diam. 19–27 cm
The British Museum
(Am1905,0216.7,9&11)

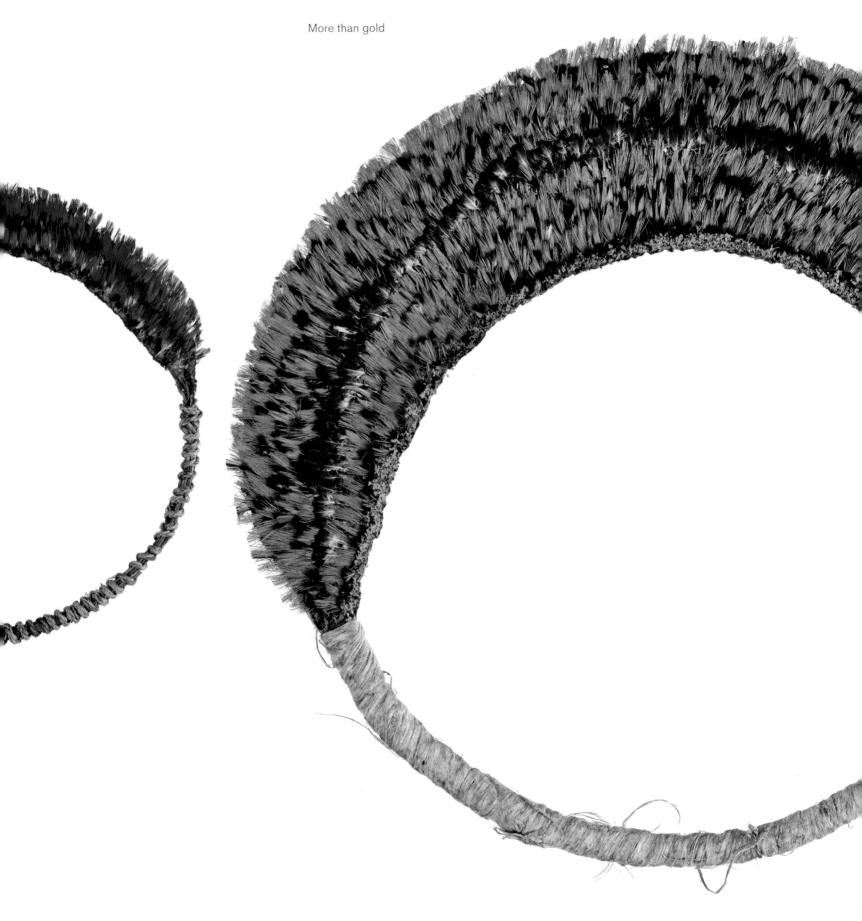

Music and ritual

Some musical instruments were probably sacred objects, brought out only on special occasions, their care and use surrounded by ritual. Colonial accounts from ancient Colombia describe sacred ceremonies where dancing, singing and the sound of trumpets and drums together with other musical instruments were a vital part of the display. Sound, decoration and movement came together as instruments reproduced the noises of the animals, spirits and other beings into which the dancers appeared to transform. This small figure appears to be dancing. He holds a staff in each hand.

Anthropomorphic pendant
1 BC – AD 700
Early Tolima
Gold alloy
H 7 cm, W 3.8 cm
Museo del Oro (O06239)

Singing was an important
way of communicating
with the supernatural and
creating harmony in the
community. These jars
have open mouths as if
singing or chanting.

Vessel
AD 600–1600
Late Nariño
Ceramic
H 10.1 cm, Diam. 12.1 cm
Museo del Oro (C03303)

Vessel
AD 600–1600
Late Nariño
Ceramic
H 14 cm, Diam. 13 cm
Museo del Oro (C09930)

Ocarinas

Ocarinas were one of the most common musical instruments used in ancient Colombia. They were probably kept as portable, personal objects. They have a hole to blow through and several finger holes to produce notes of different pitch. There are many styles with different decoration, showing how widely used they were across the region. They were often placed in burials by the mouth of the dead person, or in funerary urns.

Seashell-shaped ocarina
AD 600–1600
Late Nariño
Ceramic
H 16.7 cm, W 7.8 cm
Museo del Oro (C09896)

Jaguar-man ocarina
AD 900–1600
Tairona
Ceramic
H 7.7 cm, W 5.5 cm
Museo del Oro (C10364)

Seashell-shaped ocarina
AD 600–1600
Late Nariño
Ceramic
H 10.1 cm, W 9.6 cm
Museo del Oro (C05642)

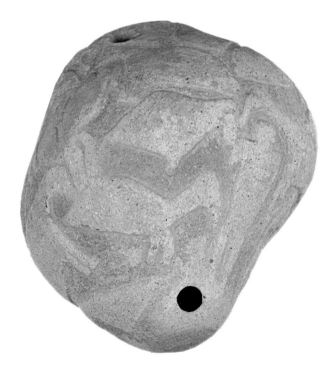

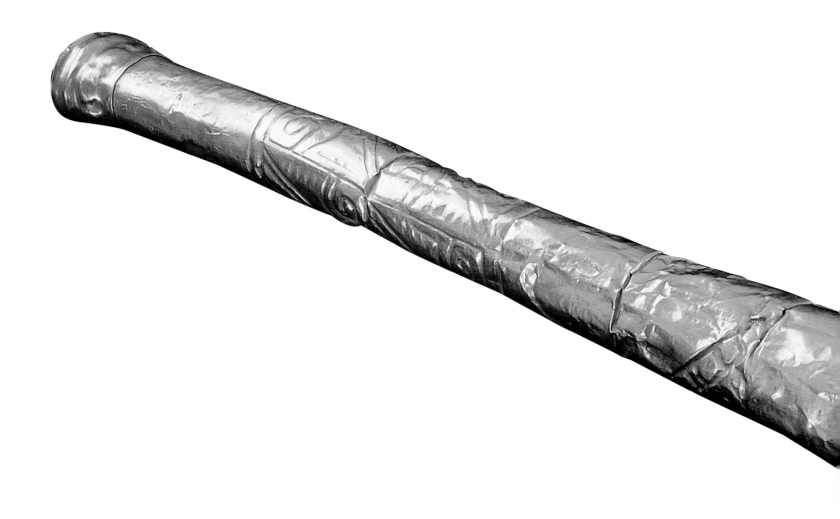

This gold trumpet-shaped instrument is made of hammered and embossed gold, clearly an object of high-status or value. It might originally have been crafted from wood or bone and then covered with the thin layer of gold.

Trumpet
200 BC – AD 1300
Calima-Malagana
(Yotoco-Malagana)
Gold alloy
L 27 cm, Diam. 4.5 cm
Museo del Oro (O06121)

Bells and rattles

Bells and rattles were probably made from several organic materials. Special ones were made from gold with cast metal pebbles or stones inside. Some bells, of different sizes and made from gold alloy, stone and other materials, were shaped as small cylinders with a vertical opening on one side and a little rim to hold them by. These were played with a beater. Chronicles also mention large drums that were played at public ceremonies.

Bell and beater
AD 900–1600
Tairona
Stone
Bell H 5 cm, W 4 cm,
D 3 cm
The British Museum
(Am1911,1213.14 & 30)

Bell
AD 900–1600
Tairona
Stone
H 10 cm, Diam. 5 cm
The British Museum
(Am1911,1213.16)

Bell
Gold alloy
AD 900–1600
Tairona
Gold alloy
H 8.5 cm, Diam. 3.6 cm
Museo del Oro (O33860)

Bell
AD 900–1600
Tairona
Gold alloy
H 3 cm, W 2 cm, D 2.5 cm
The British Museum
(Am1902.0904.8)

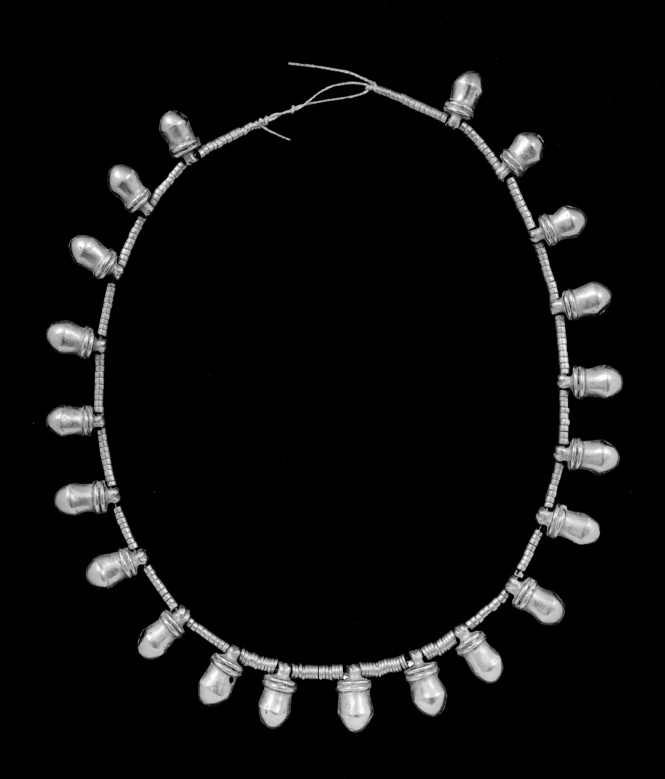

Necklace
200 BC – AD 1000
Early Zenú
Gold alloy
L 42 cm
Museo del Oro (O33716)

Small bells were often
attached to ornaments, or
strung as necklaces that
jangled and produced
rhythmic sounds as the
wearer moved. Some might
have been attached to ritual
objects or sewn into fabric.

Bell
500 BC – AD 700
Early Quimbaya
Gold alloy
H 6.3 cm, Diam. 3.8 cm
Museo del Oro (O10494)

Bell
200 BC – AD 1000
Early Zenú
Gold alloy
H 5.8 cm, Diam. 6.8 cm
Museo del Oro (O32528)

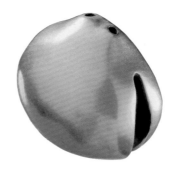

Bell
200 BC – AD 1000
Early Zenú
Gold alloy
H 7.8 cm, Diam. 5.5 cm
Museo del Oro (O17195)

Bell
AD 600–1600
Late Nariño
Gold alloy
H 3.4 cm, Diam. 4 cm
Museo del Oro (O30590)

These figures were probably made to be used during rituals. Each has a piece inside that rattles, making a different, distinctive, sound. They might have been suspended by the small openings in the shoulders and underarms, and were probably carried in ceremonies and rituals.

Figurine rattle
AD 700–1600
Late Quimbaya
Ceramic
H 26 cm, W 18 cm, D 4 cm
The British Museum
(Am1949,07.5)

Figurine rattle
AD 700–1600
Late Quimbaya
Ceramic
H 15.5 cm, W 14 cm, D 4 cm
The British Museum (WG2325)

Figurine rattle
AD 700–1600
Late Quimbaya
Ceramic
H 20 cm, W 12 cm, D 4 cm
The British Museum
(Am1896,1246)

Power and transformation

Spiritual leaders were
specialists, guardians of social
order, who were believed to
move between worlds and
transform themselves into other
forms and identities. Each
new identity brought with it a
different perspective or way
of seeing the world: as hunter,
prey, warrior, enemy or ancestor.

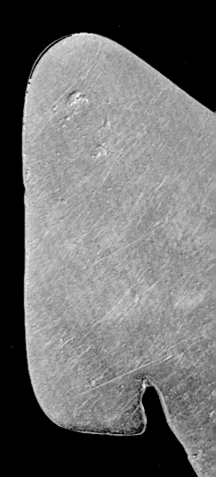

Power and transformation

Powerful chiefdoms dominated the vast and diverse ancient Colombian landscape, and maintained complex trade networks with neighbouring groups. Ruling chiefs dominated the political, social and economic spheres, while spiritual leaders advised them in important affairs as they guided the community and mediated with the supernatural. Complex training and rituals of passage legitimized those spiritual leaders and enabled them to assert their power within the community.

Rituals and warfare would have consolidated some of the dynamic relationships between neighbouring groups and within a community, while also playing an important role in the negotiations and relationships with the divine. The various types of surviving weaponry, including clubs, javelins, bows, arrows, spear-throwers (see pp. 124–5) and lances, together with protective gear such as helmets (see pp. 123–4), breastplates and shields, testify to the battles that took place centuries ago. Some of those objects crafted in gold not only became public displays of power before the community and a clear threat to the enemy, but also would have imbued the wearers with the strength and protection of the supernatural.

Battles were highly symbolic and ritualized in ancient America, and in some instances, victory on the battlefield was publicly flaunted through the practice of trophy headhunting (see pp. 120–1). As the Spanish chronicler Gonzalo Fernandez de Oviedo describes, 'If the men of Bogotá kill or take any Panches Indians prisoner, they take the heads back to their homeland and put them in their oratories'.[1] The Muisca, in one type of ritual, sacrificed young boys by shooting arrows at them while they were tied to the tops of posts. In some other instances, captives were given as sacrificial offerings to the gods in special locations, such as mountain tops and other ceremonial places. Such rituals, which are particularly alien to modern Western sensibilities, testify to the very different cosmovision and relationship with the supernatural world adopted by ancient Colombian peoples.

Chiefs and spiritual leaders were given the responsibility of protecting their community, and ensuring its health and wellbeing. In order to allow them to connect with the supernatural and venture into the spiritual world, ritual and transformative practices (both physical and spiritual) were necessary. One such practice, restricted to the elites and initiated specialists, involved the ingestion of

1. Oviedo 1536–9, p. 73.

2. Ibid.

3. This was one of the earliest plants to be domesticated in the New World: its use can be attested in South America 8,000 years ago.

4. Coca leaves are rich in vitamins C, B1 and riboflavin; they also contain high levels of calcium and iron. Chewing them may have prevented scurvy in regions where fruit and vegetables were in short supply.

5. Cieza de León 1864, p. 352.

Tunjo (votive figure)
AD 600–1600
Muisca
Gold alloy
H 6.8 cm, W 2.3 cm
Museo del Oro (O29284)

enhancing and hallucinogenic substances to facilitate communication with the supernatural. As Oviedo describes:

> They will not set out, nor make war, nor undertake anything important without knowing how the affair will turn out.… They say that the sun will tell them how they should proceed in what they ask. And if you ask them how the sun tells them this, after they have taken certain herbs, they reply that if certain joints move after the Indians have eaten herbs, it is a sign that their affairs or their wishes will come out well. And if certain other joints move, it is a sign that things will not turn out well, but badly.[2]

Spiritual leaders were consulted by the elites as well as the community at large. They acted as healers and advisors, and would embark on transformative soul journeys that allowed them to take on the attitude and appearance of different animals. Their knowledge of their natural surroundings, together with their lengthy and specialized training, allowed them to smoke, ingest or snuff a wide variety of plants, the use of which would have been forbidden to the rest of the community. Those substances enabled them to set off on mystical soul flights to other dimensions of the universe in order to communicate with ancestors and spirits, and see and understand the world from another perspective.

One of the plants that was considered sacred, its use carefully managed within these societies, was coca (*Erythroxylum novogranatense*).[3] It was chewed and used as a stimulant, but also made up for certain elements lacking in some diets at this time.[4] As Cieza de León noted: 'When I asked some of these Indians why they carried these leaves in their mouths (which they do not eat, but merely hold between their teeth), they reply that it prevents them from feeling hungry, and gives them vigour and strength.'[5] Coca was chewed to heighten physical endurance, particularly on the battlefield and during long working hours at cold high-altitude locations.

Sumptuous and elaborate gold and *tumbaga* objects were crafted for use in these rituals. Coca was kept and carried either in special bags made of organic material or, in exceptional cases, in portable containers made of *tumbaga* (see p. 130). The leaves were chewed and a wad of coca was kept in the cheek for sucking on (see p. 131). To facilitate the absorption of the stimulants, the leaves were combined with an alkaline substance (usually powdered calcium carbonate, provided mainly by powdered lime or crushed seashells). This highly valued powder was kept in containers called *poporos*, the simplest ones made from gourds and some of the most remarkable examples fully crafted in gold alloy (see pp. 74–5 and 134–7). Dippers were used to transfer the alkaline powder to the mouth. Some exceptional examples were cast in gold alloy, and display uniquely crafted miniature figures and scenes at their end (see pp. 138–9). Gold-alloy *poporos* and dippers,[6] reserved for high-ranking individuals, display elaborate symbolic iconography and show highly skilled craftsmanship, while also publicly marking the status of the owner.

Other substances from different parts of the region, such as tobacco (*Nicotina tabacum*), yopo (*Anadenanthera peregrine* or *Piptadenia peregrina*)[7] and yajé (*Banisteriopsis caapi*), were snuffed, smoked, drunk, chewed or eaten. The snuffing of such substances by the elite is attested by the archaeological record: elaborate tumbaga snuffing tablets (see p. 140) and tubes have been found in graves across Colombia.

The use of these hallucinogenic substances taught spiritual leaders the key elements for an understanding of the universe, inducing a state of trance which made the invisible visible.

Some of those plants were believed to be food for the gods and were offered to them in ritual practices. They were imbued with various types of powers that gave them their healing, transformative and teaching properties; they were also considered to be fundamental instruments of transformation. Several practices, such as fasting, deprivation of light, as well as music and dancing, would have accompanied the ritual ingestion of such substances; the physical appearance of the person and their relation with the sensory world would have changed considerably. Visions would lead to the transformation of spiritual leaders; on their mystical soul journeys they would encounter or metamorphose into a series of animal spirits that inhabited the world and coexisted with the community. Birds, bats, felines, amphibians, snakes and alligators were just some of the powerful disguises adopted by those spirits (see 142–59). Representations of these animals were frequently made in elaborate gold pieces, denoting the important role they played in the well-being of the community and their association with the elites. Gold objects, including nose, lip and ear ornaments, diadems, pectorals and pendants, enabled a person's physical transformation, together with paint, animal pelts, feathers, as well as the use of body binding, scarifications and piercings. Each new identity achieved by a person or initiated specialist brought with it a different perspective on the world, allowing for a multifaceted knowledge of the cosmos.

The goldsmiths who were able to turn lumps of the brilliant metal into symbolically charged objects had a power at their command that resembled that of their spiritual and political leaders. This was the power of transformation that connected the worlds of humans, animals and divine

6. *Poporos* were a mark of manhood: the container represented the womb, while the lime dipper was seen as a phallic symbol.

7. Yopo, a substance prepared from the toasted and crushed seeds of a leguminous tree, has been used as a hallucinogen in South America for over 4,000 years.

8. Nicholas Saunders, '"Catching the Light": Technologies of Power and Enchantment in Pre-Columbian Goldworking', in Quilter and Hoopes 2003, p. 26.

beings. It was believed that this process of constant negotiation between the different realms ultimately helped to keep the world in order.[8] The craftsmen continually produced new gold objects; these were not intended to be hoarded and passed down through the generations, but had life cycles of their own, either accompanying their owners to their tombs or, as in the case of the Muisca, passing on to a new set of divine owners in the most powerful gestures of sacrifice.

Lobster-man pendant
200 BC – AD 1000
Early Zenú
Gold alloy
H 11.1 cm, W 7.1 cm
Museo del Oro (O32696)

Trophy headhunting

Headhunting was one of the
ritual practices associated
with warfare. The figure on
the right holds weapons, and
a decapitated head in his left
hand, perhaps symbolizing
victory on the battlefield. The
other two figures represent
the poles to which sacrificial
victims were tied.

Tunjos (votive figures)
AD 600–1600
Muisca
Gold alloy
H 11.9 cm, W 3.2 cm
H 8.9 cm, W 1.5 cm
H 7.1 cm, W 4.9 cm
Museo del Oro (O00296,
O02179, O06730)

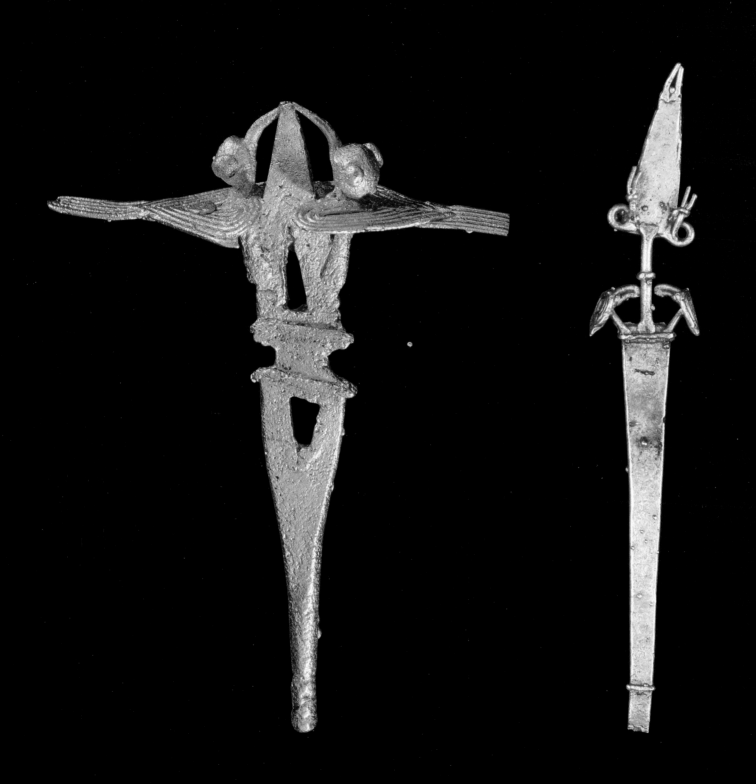

Warrior helmets

These helmets were made
from hammered gold alloy,
decorated with figures and
geometric patterns. The
soft nature of gold means
that these impressive
helmets were not made to
protect the wearer in battle.
Instead the shining gold,
reflecting the light, would
have marked the status of
the wearer and symbolically
strengthened him with the
power of the sun.

Helmets
500 BC – AD 700
Early Quimbaya
Gold alloy
H 11 cm, W 17 cm D 20 cm
H 12 cm, W 17 cm, D 20 cm
The British Museum
(Am1910,1202.1; Am+342)

Spear-throwers

Warriors in ancient
Colombia used a wide range
of weapons, including spear-
throwers. They set a dart
or spear into the handle,
which gave them greater
reach and helped them to
throw the dart with greater
force. Many highly decorated
handles, such as these, were
cast in gold alloy by skilled
goldsmiths. The imagery
and material show they were
highly valued items, perhaps
used as scepters to display
status as well as in battle.

Spear-thrower finial
500 BC – AD 700
Early Quimbaya
Gold alloy
H 12 cm, W 2 cm, D 4 cm
The British Museum
(Am1910,1202.10)

Spear-thrower
Gold alloy
200 BC – AD 1300
Calima-Malagana
(Yotoco-Malagana)
L 29.7 cm, Diam. 4 cm
Museo del Oro (O29068)

Tunjos (votive figures)
AD 600–1600
Muisca
Gold alloy
H 8.3 cm, W 3.3 cm
H 5.9 cm, W 3.5 cm
H 8 cm, W 4.2 cm
H 11.6 cm, W 6.1 cm
H 9.9 cm, W 3.3 cm
H 12 cm, W 3 cm
Museo del Oro (O23648,
O29025, O06755, O03046,
O32812, O06365)

Male figures

Members of the elite were often shown
seated on stools or benches. This symbolized
their wisdom, balance, power and status.
In a seated position, spiritual leaders were
believed to be more connected with the
cosmos and able to communicate with
ancestors and spirits. The standing warrior
figures wear headdresses and carry weapons
as symbols of their power and strength. Such
objects were buried or placed in significant
places in the landscape to seek favour from or
give thanks to the gods.

Anthropomorphic pendants
500 BC – AD 700
Early Quimbaya
Gold alloy
H 7 cm, W 7 cm
H 8.5 cm, W 6.4 cm
Museo del Oro (O03492,
O06031)

These highly decorated cast figures are holding sticks to their mouths. They may be masked and the spiral shapes may represent wings or ornaments, possibly illustrating people engaged in a ritual or in transformation. As for many of these figures, their meaning remains a mystery.

Ritual coca-chewing

Various objects were used
in ritual coca-chewing. The
ceramic figure shows a
person sitting on a stool,
with a wad of coca leaf in
his cheek. Coca leaves
were usually stored in bags.
Occasionally they were kept
in a container such as the
fine, smooth gold vessel on
the right.

Coca leaf container
500 BC – AD 700
Early Quimbaya
Gold alloy
H 21.4 cm, W 10.5 cm
Museo del Oro (O32853)

Seated male figure
AD 600–1600
Late Nariño
Ceramic
H 17.5 cm, W 12.5 cm
Museo del Oro (C12632)

Lime flasks

The coca leaves by themselves had little effect, but when mixed in the mouth with lime powder or mineral lime, made from crushed shells, they acted as a mild stimulant. The lime was kept in flasks known as *poporos* and extracted using a dipping pin. The most elaborate *poporos* were crafted in gold alloy, sometimes mimicking the shape of natural gourds, from which simpler *poporos* were often made.

Poporo (lime container) in the shape of a fruit
500 BC – AD 700
Early Quimbaya
Gold alloy
H 16.7 cm, Diam. 8.6 cm
Museo del Oro (O02995)

Poporo (lime container)
AD 300–1600
Urabá
Gold alloy
H 14.3 cm, Diam. 6 cm
Museo del Oro (O33041)

Some lime flasks were made of two parts – a container and a neck. This highly decorated neck with six identical cast faces is one of the most striking surviving examples of its kind. It would have been attached to a natural gourd. The opening at the top would have been used to insert the lime dipper.

Poporo (lime container) neck
500 BC – AD 700
Early Quimbaya
Gold alloy
H 17 cm, Diam. 8 cm
The British Museum
(Am1940,11.1)

Calima goldsmiths created
small figurative *poporos*,
for instance in the shape
of humans and animals,
from hammered sheets of
gold. The face here has
a nose ring with a green
bead – a mark of high status.
Sometimes holes on either
side suggest they were
suspended and worn.

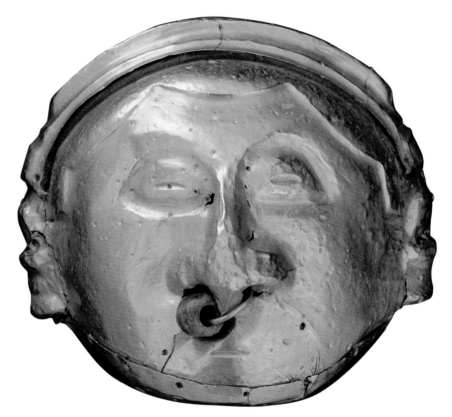

Poporo
(lime container)
Gold alloy
200 BC – AD 1300
Calima-Malagana
(Yotoco-Malagana)
H 5.3 cm, W 6.3 cm
Museo del Oro (O32851)

Bird-shaped *poporo*
(lime container)
200 BC – AD 1300
Calima-Malagana
(Yotoco-Malagana)
Gold alloy
H 19 cm, W 6 cm
Museo del Oro (O33571)

Lime dipping pins

Dippers were used to extract lime from a container, to enhance the stimulating effect produced by chewing coca leaves. They were licked first so that the fine powder would stick to them. They would then be placed again in the mouth to mix the powder with the wad of leaves. Calima goldsmiths decorated the tops of dipping pins with intricately cast miniature figures and scenes. The time and skill invested in making them shows their importance in the ritual consumption of coca leaves.

Lime dippers with anthropomorphic and zoomorphic finials
200 BC – AD 1300
Calima-Malagana
(Yotoco-Malagana)
Gold alloy
H 22–30.5 cm, W 1–2.5 cm
Museo del Oro (O03453, O02975, O04252, O05128, O07534, O03454)

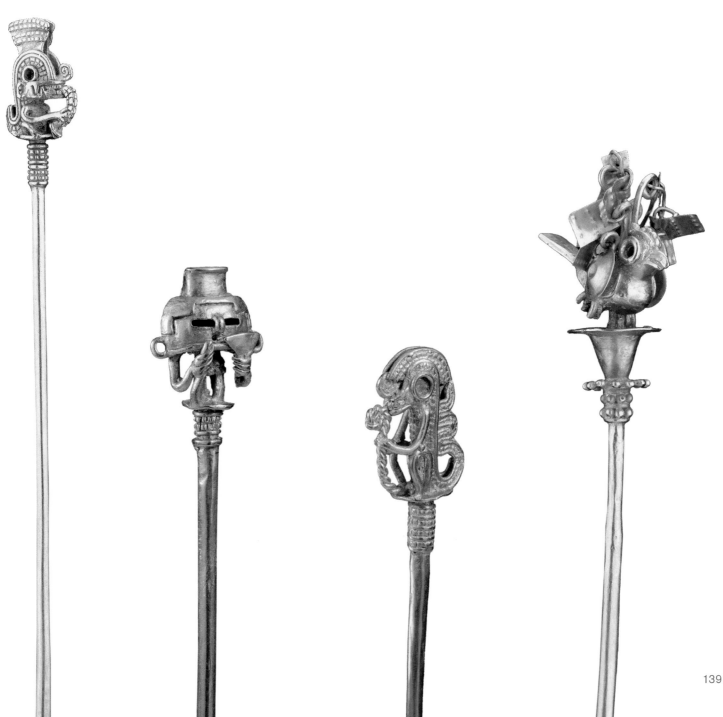

Ritual snuffing trays

Powerful hallucinogenic substances such as yopo were produced from dried or crushed plant seeds. They were sniffed or swallowed to induce visions and aid communication with the supernatural world. Their use was highly restricted to initiated specialists and spiritual leaders.

Snuffing trays
AD 600–1600
Muisca
Gold alloy
L 10.1 cm, W 1.6 cm
L 6.1 cm, W 2 cm
Museo del Oro (O06914, O08479)

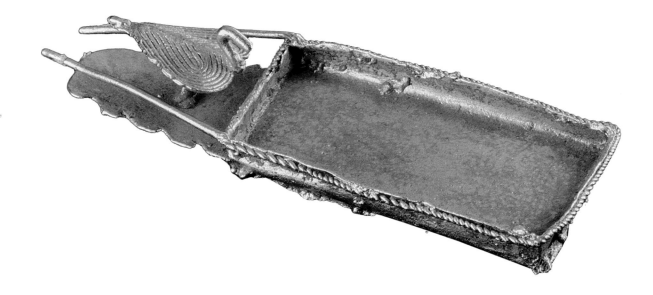

Figures with masks

Spiritual leaders believed they could travel the universe and negotiate with spirits by transforming themselves into different creatures. Wearing masks transformed not only a person's appearance but also their identity, probably giving them special powers.

Tunjos (votive figures)
AD 600–1600
Muisca
Gold alloy
H 6.6 cm, W 2.4 cm
H 7.5 cm, W 2.7 cm
Museo del Oro (O28695, O32958)

Animals and transformations

Many creatures in ancient Colombia had symbolic power for the communities that lived there. Craftspeople copied their shapes to decorate ritual objects, often in stylized and abstract forms, or represented by a single characteristic feature.

Tairona artisans created necklaces made of frog-shaped beads (opposite) that would have rattled as they were worn, perhaps representing the sound of these creatures. Frogs belonged on land and in water and were especially common in rainforest areas. Warriors might have added the poison from the coloured skin of some frogs to the tips of their arrows.

Monkeys were often represented in groups as in these ear decorations (above right). Monkeys can jump long distances from tree to tree, in spectacular leaps that look like flight, and so were associated with the world of the sky.

Pair of earrings with
monkeys
AD 600–1600
Late Nariño
Gold alloy
H 8.5 cm, W 10.9 cm
Museo del Oro (O25405,
O25406)

Necklace with frogs
AD 900–1600
Tairona
Gold alloy, stone
Each frog H 2.1 cm,
W 1.5 cm
Museo del Oro (O13218)

The people in Muisca territory produced votive *tunjo* figurines in the shape of snakes. Others, like the Calima and Tairona, represented humans transforming into snakes. These creatures were linked to darkness and the underworld. They live on land and water and can jump through the air to strike their prey, and so were seen as intermediaries between the worlds of land, water and sky. Snakes also shed their skins and this might have been symbolic of renewal and regeneration.

Snake *tunjos* (votive offerings)
AD 600–1600
Muisca
Gold alloy
H 0.5 cm, W 2 cm, L 10 cm; H 2.5 cm, W 3 cm, L 15.5 cm
The British Museum
(Am7461, Am1949,07.1)

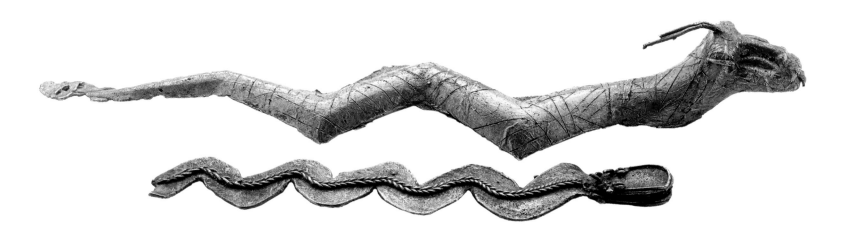

Lobster-man pendant
AD 300–1600
Urabá
Gold alloy
H 8.5 cm, W 4.3 cm
Museo del Oro (O33381)

Lobsters and crabs
may have been seen as
mediators between the
worlds of land and water.
This stylized pendant
combines human features
with lobster claws and a tail
(see also p.119).

Goldsmiths have represented these two crocodiles or caimans with rough skin and sharp teeth. These reptiles dominated life in rivers, which were seen as connecting this world with the underworld. Crocodiles with their rough skin, lying motionless in the water, may also have represented the earth floating in a mythical sea.

Crocodile shaped pendants
700 BC – AD 1600
Late Quimbaya
Gold alloy
L 7.9 cm, W 3 cm
L 30 cm, W 6 cm
Museo del Oro (O05928, O06811)

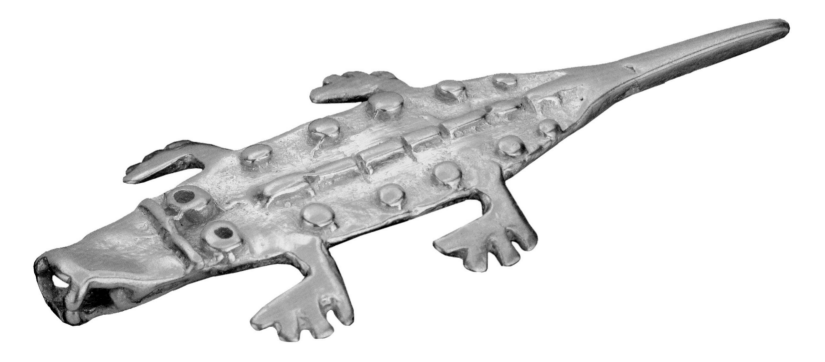

Jaguars are the largest predators in South America, known for their ferocity and strength. They can walk silently in the forest, run long distances and see their prey in the dark.

Across South America they were associated with rulers and power. Chiefs and spiritual leaders would symbolically transform themselves into jaguars, for instance by wearing their skins, or masks with menacing fangs or necklaces with fierce claws.

Goldsmiths also made many representations of these creatures, probably for ritual use. They were associated with the sun, with thunder and fire, because of their golden colour.

Feline figurine
AD 600–1600
Muisca
Gold alloy
H 1.5 cm, W 2.5 cm, D 1 cm
The British Museum (Am,S1329)

Feline figurine
200 BC – AD 1000
Early Zenú
Ceramic
H 9.6 cm, W 7.5 cm, L 18.6 cm
Museo del Oro (C12820)

Feline ornament
200 BC – AD 1300
Calima-Malagana
(Yotoco-Malagana)
Gold alloy
H 9.2 cm, W 12.8 cm
Museo del Oro (O33223)

There are many species of birds in Colombia, from powerful predator eagles and water birds to the tiny hummingbird. These and others were represented in ancient Colombia, some in great detail, others by particular characteristics, such as a long beak, spread wings or feathered tails. Their ability to fly, their powerful beaks and claws, iridescent and colourful plumage and constant singing and movement made them perfect symbols of the upper world, of supernatural power and transformation.

Bird pectoral
AD 900–1600
Tairona
Gold alloy
H 9.1 cm, W 6.6 cm
Museo del Oro (O14525)

Bird-man pectoral
AD 900–1600
Late Cauca
Gold alloy
H 16.5 cm,
W 13.3 cm, D.2.1 cm
Museo del Oro (O06414)

Gold ornaments in the shape
of birds with spread wings
are believed to show the
ecstatic flight of spiritual
leaders, who with the help
of chanting, ritual dancing
and hallucinogenic plants
experienced imaginary
long distance flights to
see the world from another
perspective, to discover the
cure for diseases and to
acquire knowledge.

Bird-shaped staff finial
200 BC – AD 1000
Early Zenú
Gold alloy
H 4.5 cm, W 2.7 cm,
L 10.5 cm
Museo del Oro (O33449)

Bird-shaped pectoral
AD 600–1600
Late Nariño
Gold alloy
H 9 cm, W 11.7 cm
Museo del Oro (O22451)

Anthropomorphic
bat-man pectoral
AD 900–1600
Tairona
Gold alloy
H 9.5 cm, W 11.9 cm
Museo del Oro (O16584)

The representation of
bats ranges from intricate,
decorated pieces to very
abstract, stylized shapes.

Bats were associated with
night and the underworld.
They are efficient hunters
and some feed on the
blood of larger prey. Tairona
craftsmen, especially, made
fabulous representations of
bats and bat-men, as well
as body ornaments for the
members of the elite. These
physically transformed
the wearer's appearance
and included gold visors,
together with nose and lip
ornaments that would have
left permanent marks on
the skin. By wearing such
ornaments during rituals,
spiritual leaders believed
their spirits could take on
the strength, agility in flight
and night vision of bats
themselves.

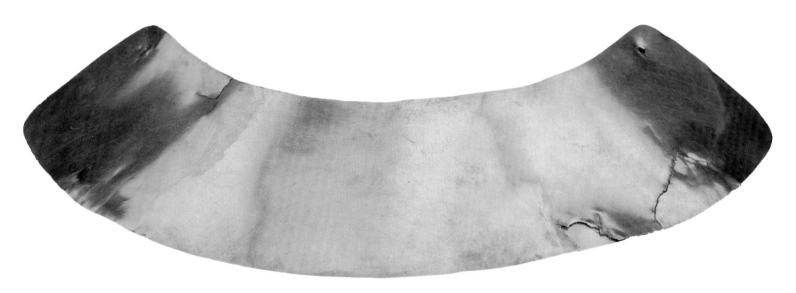

Visor
AD 900–1600
Tairona
Gold alloy
H 4.8 cm, W 21.2 cm,
Museo del Oro (O14366)

Nose ornaments
AD 900–1600
Tairona
Gold alloy
L 11 cm, Diam. 1.7 cm
L 10.9 cm, Diam. 2.4 cm
Museo del Oro (O14629,
O16034)

Lip ornament
AD 900–1600
Tairona
Gold alloy
H 2 cm, W 4 cm
Museo del Oro (O20468)

Anthropomorphic
bat-man staff finial
AD 900–1600
Tairona
Gold alloy
H 6 cm, W 2.5 cm
Museo del Oro (O26176)

This small bat-man figure is
wearing head, nose and lip
ornaments similar to those
illustrated opposite.

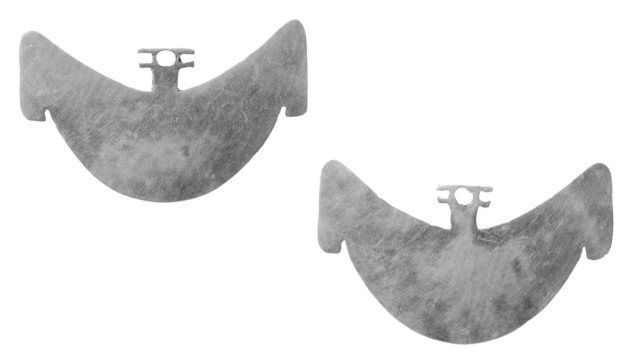

Pair of bat-shaped earrings
1 BC – AD 700
Early Tolima
Gold alloy
Each H 5.5 cm, W 9.2 cm
Museo del Oro (O05714,
O05715)

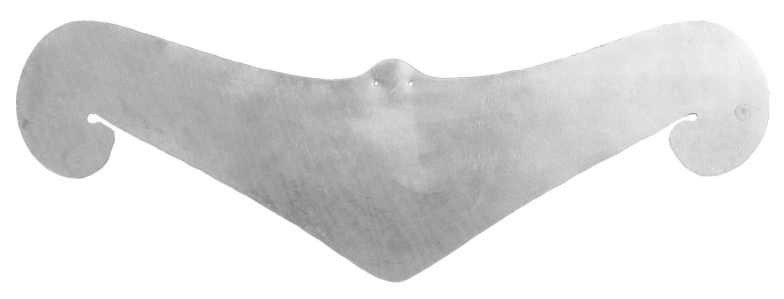

Bat-shaped pectoral
200 BC – AD 1300
Calima-Malagana
(Yotoco-Malagana)
Gold alloy
H 11.1 cm, W 33.1 cm
Museo del Oro (O33412)

Life and death

Across ancient Colombia there were many different forms of burial practice and rituals surrounding death. Communities spent much time and effort in creating impressive burial sites that would ensure the status and well-being of the deceased for eternity.

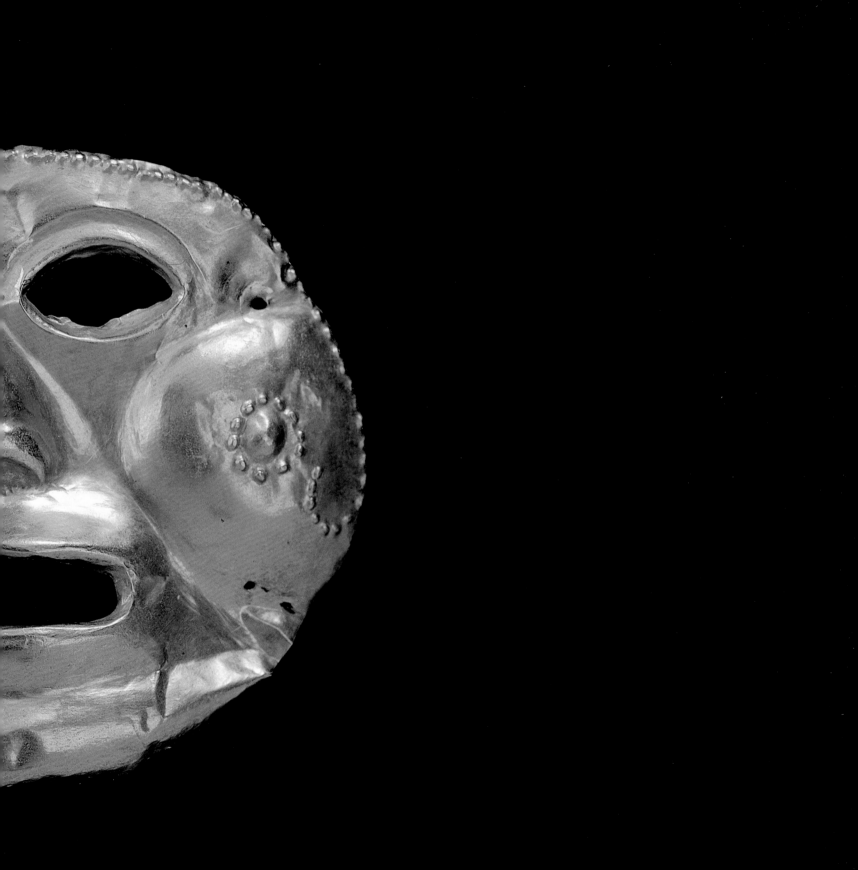

Life and death

Life and death were viewed as a continuum in Andean cosmovision. During ceremonies involving feasting, drinking, music and dancing the deceased were celebrated and repeatedly revisited, incorporated in the life and festivities of the living. Elites were buried with elaborate rituals that would have strengthened the social links within communities and between groups spread over a large territory. As a result of the many different chiefdoms and ethnic groups that existed in ancient Colombia, treatment of the deceased and burial practices varied hugely from community to community.

Since early times in ancient America much time and effort was invested in creating elaborate burial sites that would ensure the status and well-being of the deceased for eternity. Among early ancient Colombian cultures San Agustín shows unique examples of complex burials, including monumental stone-carving and monolithic sarcophagi housed in semi-subterranean chambers that were once colourfully decorated. Anthropomorphic figures, once painted in bright colours, guarded the entrances to these chambers. They were a constant reminder of the effort invested in safeguarding the deceased in their final resting place. In Tierradentro there are impressive necropolises where elaborately painted burial chambers, accessed by complex staircases, led to an underworld where the dead were accompanied by their retainers and wealth for the afterlife.

In other communities, such as the Muisca, some bodies were intentionally dried close to a fire and wrapped in consecutive layers of fine textiles, a funerary practice that was provided only to those of the highest social class. Kept in a flexed position, they were deposited in caves, rock shelters, funerary chambers and other solitary locations. High-status individuals, mostly chiefs and spiritual leaders, would have sat on chairs and benches, known as *tiangas*, during their lifetime to show their rank, wisdom and social position within the community. Some of these seats have also been found in burials, extending the status of the sitter to their new life. A chronicle mentions that when a cacique died, 'They prepare him for burial on a *tianga*, which is a stool that the chieftains sit on, and they dance around him … and afterwards they bury him, still seated on his *tianga*'.[1] In other instances, smaller than life-size chairs have been found by archaeologists, probably mimicking those used in life but in smaller formats specially crafted to accompany the deceased in his or her

1. Paz Maldonado 1582.

San Agustin sculpture with remaining traces of paint. Originally they would have been painted in bright colours.

Painted walls, ceiling and pillars in the interior of an underground tomb at Tierradentro

resting place (see pp. 168–9). Seats and benches were symbols of stability and wisdom, and so sitting down was equated with thought, equilibrium and power.

Some people, including those in the Tolima region, considered the bones of the deceased to be the seeds of new life and secondary burials were therefore common. In some instances the flesh was left to decay, or the corpse was smoked dry and the bones later collected, sometimes ritually burned and deposited in large funerary urns together with offerings. Both individual and collective burials have been found inside these ceramics containers, and some Tolima and other burial sites revealed several urns deposited together. An entourage including family members and slaves most probably accompanied the principal figure in his final journey and was sacrificed alongside him. In those instances the identity of the deceased and his fate in the afterlife were combined with the fate of the wider community. The interment of those urns in burial chambers, caves and chosen locations allowed the deceased to take their final journey into the world of the dead, and symbolized the end of a ritual that might have lasted days, months, sometimes even years.

San Agustín sculptural group at the entrance of a semi-subterranean tomb.

Other people, such as those in the Calima-Malagana and the Quimbaya regions, in some instances placed the body in a stretched-out position. The deceased would have been wrapped in fine textiles and full regalia, and placed in tombs including shaft graves, shaft and chamber tombs, and funerary mounds. Finally they were covered with earthen or stone tumuli, stones or shards, depending on the different funerary practices. In the most elaborate burials, a large and varied array of goods was placed in the tombs, including valuable materials such as gold and fine textiles, stones, and other necessities such as food and drink.

The chronicler Fernández de Oviedo describes how gold and finery were placed next to the deceased in their final resting places, and how the body was treated in one community:

> In the area of Tunja, leading figures and other prominent captains are not buried, as I will now explain. They place their bodies, with all the gold they possess, in their shrines and houses of prayer, on certain beds that the Spaniards there call 'barbacoas', which are platforms raised above the ground on stakes, and they leave them there with all their riches either stuck to the dead body or placed near it.[2]

2. Oviedo 1535.

164

Other chroniclers, such as Pedro Sarmiento, describe in more detail some of these complex rituals, from the preparation of the body, including the use of gold worn by the deceased together with the use of cotton cloth made specifically for wrapping the body for burial. He also describes the sacrificial objects deposited in the tomb that enabled the deceased to continue his new life in accordance with the status and traditions to which he was accustomed. Communication with the deceased, he explains, was not lost and the revisiting of the tomb might have allowed the ancestor to transmit his wisdom to the living from the other world:

> The way they have of burying someone like a lord when he dies is in the countryside, somewhere hidden.... First they put him on a raised platform with two fires burning to dry the body ... and then, when he is very dry, they put his beads on his arms and legs, and all the jewels he wore at festivities when he was alive, and they wrap him in many cotton blankets that they have kept specially for this purpose for a long time ... and then they take him to the grave they have prepared and kill two of the Indians that used to serve him, and place one at his feet and the other at his head. The grave is very deep, and inside it is a great vault which is closed off with sticks that do not rot.... In there they place his weapons and the seats he used to sit on and the cups he used to drink out of and goblets full of wine and plates full of the delicacies he used to eat, and they say that they do this so he can eat at night, and they listen above the grave for many days to see if they can hear him.[3]

Most of the gold and *tumbaga* objects that have survived to this day (with the exception of the unique Muisca votive offerings) were deposited in elaborate tombs. Some of these show signs of continuous use during life, being personal ritual objects or precious adornments that asserted the identity and status of the wearer. Only a few examples might have been commissioned specifically for the adornment of the deceased, including textiles and impressive masks (see pp. 178–81) that were placed over the face of the deceased or at their feet in the final burial place.

As a result of the effort invested by the community in preserving the memory of these individuals for eternity and ensuring their well-being in the afterlife, we are now able to enjoy these magnificent pieces, and learn more about the fascinating people that used and created them.

3. Sarmiento 1540.

Stone guardian

This fanged figure would once have been brightly painted. Pointed jaguar teeth mark his relationship with the spirit and supernatural world. He is armed with a shield and club, representing strength and a fearless nature. Such sculptures guarded the final resting place of high-status individuals from harmful spirits and enemies.

Tomb guardian figure
AD 1–900
San Agustín
Stone
H 102 cm, W 36 cm,
D 20 cm
The British Museum
(Am1899,1012.1)

Funerary chair
1 BC – AD 700
Early Tolima
Ceramic
H 42.2 cm, W 22.4 cm
Museo del Oro (C00895)

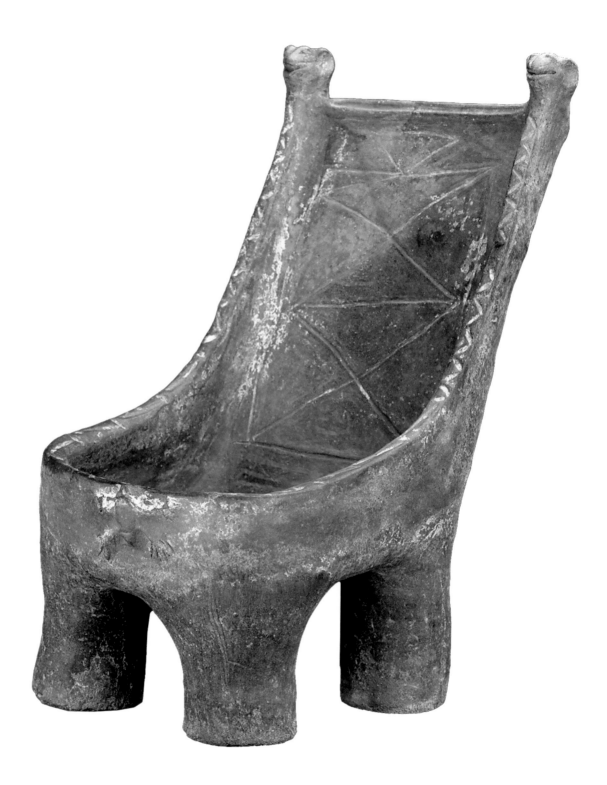

Funerary chairs

In life, chairs and stools
in ancient Colombia
were symbols of stability,
knowledge and wisdom, and
were used only by elites,
including rulers and spiritual
leaders. When someone
of high status died, some
communities wrapped the
crouched body in layers
of fine cloth and placed it
in a chair to maintain the
person's status in the next
life. Miniature chairs were
also placed next to bodies,
perhaps to be used by the
spirits of the dead. Some
funerary urns show people
seated in chairs or on
stools, representing their
high status.

Urn with seated figure
AD 900–1600
Late Middle Magdalena
Ceramic
H 55.5 cm, Diam. 37.5 cm
Museo del Oro (C00835)

Burial urns

Urns held the remains of the dead, sometimes of more than one person. Many societies in ancient Colombia buried their dead in what is known as secondary burials. Once the flesh had decayed or dried the bones were either burned or collected and placed in a large urn along with offerings of gold and other objects.

Urns were placed in burial chambers, caves or other chosen sites. This signified the person's final step into the world of the dead.

Urn with seated figure
AD 900–1600
Late Middle Magdalena
Ceramic
H 93.5 cm, Diam. 36.3 cm
Museo del Oro (C00786)

Anthropomorphic urn
1 BC – AD 700
Early Tolima
Ceramic
H 38.8 cm, Diam. 40 cm
Museo del Oro (C01235)

Anthropomorphic urn
AD 1000–1600
Tamalameque
Ceramic
H 70.4 cm, Diam. 30.5 cm
Museo del Oro (C02035)

Chest ornaments and masks

In some cultures, the bodies of high-ranking dignitaries were wrapped in cloth and buried in a stretched-out position. They were placed in graves and tombs, often accompanied by valuable materials such as gold, textiles and stones, as well as food and drink. The community believed the power of the gold would help their leaders retain their special status in the afterlife. Most of the gold objects placed in burials would also have been used by the deceased in life.

Pectoral
Gold alloy
200 BC – AD 1300
Calima-Malagana
(Yotoco-Malagana)
Gold alloy
H 37.3 cm, W 47.7 cm
Museo del Oro (O33336)

Pectoral (necklace and nose
ring later additions)
200 BC – AD 1300
Calima Malagana
(Yotoco-Malagana)
Gold alloy
H 28 cm, W 37 cm, D 6 cm
The British Museum
(Am1900,0517.1)

This spectacular hammered mask with a dangling nose ornament would probably have been placed on top of the face of a funerary bundle – the wrapped body of the deceased – transforming him into an ancestor and semi-divine figure.

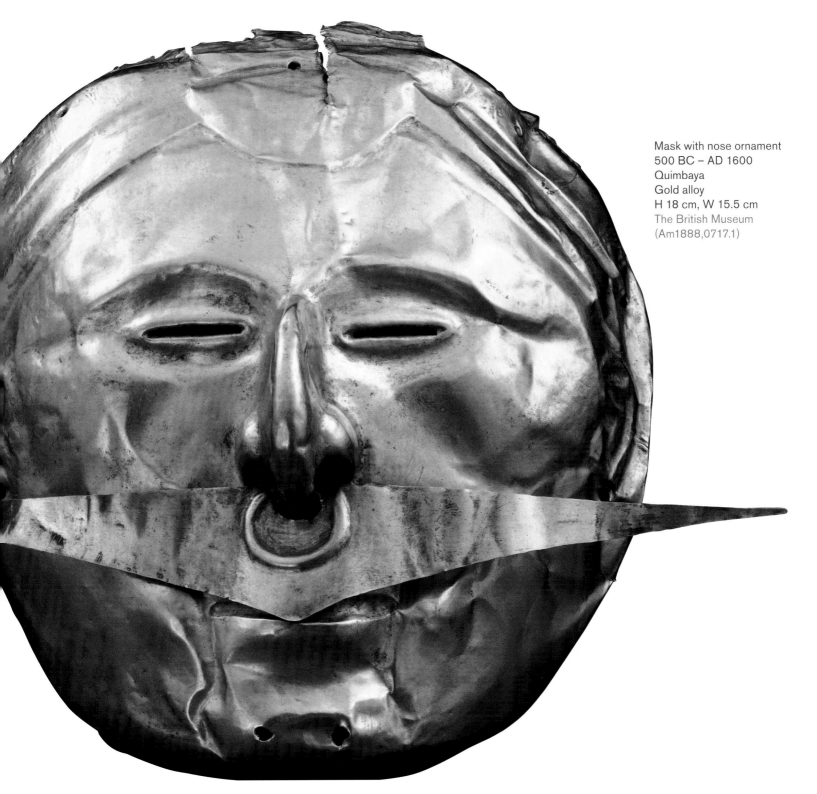

Mask with nose ornament
500 BC – AD 1600
Quimbaya
Gold alloy
H 18 cm, W 15.5 cm
The British Museum
(Am1888,0717.1)

Funerary mask
200 BC – AD 1300
Calima-Malagana
(Yotoco-Malagana)
Gold alloy
H 28.8 cm, W 38 cm
Museo del Oro (O33194)

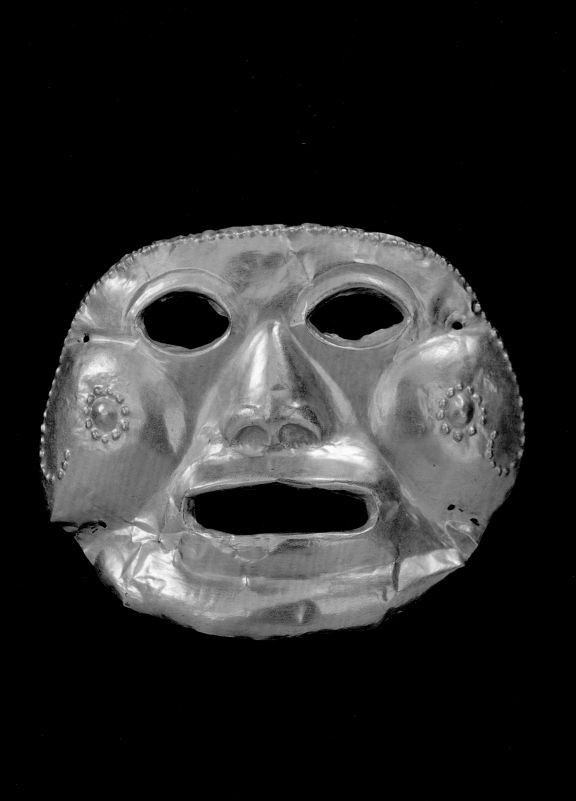

Some large masks may have been made specifically for burial. They vary in style from naturalistic faces, with volume and detail, through to examples with minimal representation of facial features. Perhaps such stylised masks alluded to the individual's transformation from the material to the spiritual world. In some excavated tombs, faces have been covered by three masks, layered one on top of another.

Funerary mask
1600 BC – AD 100
Calima-Malagana (Ilama)
Gold alloy
H 13.5 cm, W 16 cm
Museo del Oro (O03883)

Glossary

Alloy

A substance formed from the combination of a metal with one or more other metals or non-metallic materials.

Anthropomorphic

A term used to describe the attribution of human characteristics to non-human beings or inanimate objects. From Greek *anthropomorphos* ('human form').

Burnishing

A method of smoothing and polishing the surface of a metal or ceramic object by rubbing with another object.

Cacique

A term derived from the Caribbean Taino language which was appropriated by the Spaniards of the colonial era to designate indigenous leaders within their West Indian and other Latin American territories.

Cercado

Spanish: 'enclosure'. Among people in the Muisca region, the fenced settlement of a chief containing a ceremonial centre as well as ordinary dwellings.

Chiefdom

A socio-political unit consisting of several communities whose leaders recognise the authority of one paramount chief or kin group.

Coca

A plant of the family *Erythroxylaceae* from western South America that has been cultivated by indigenous people since pre-Columbian times for its stimulating and hunger- and thirst-quenching qualities and perceived divine origin.

Copper oxidization

The chemical process in which copper reacts with the oxygen contained in the air to form a greenish layer on its surface (patina).

Cosmovision

A particular way of viewing the world or of understanding the universe; especially in Literary Criticism or with reference to Meso-American peoples.

Diffusion bonding

A welding technique in which two metal surfaces are joined through the application of high temperatures and pressure and without the help of any fillers.

False filigree

A term used to describe objects which resemble filigree work but which are in fact created using the lost-wax casting process, the original model being built up from wire-like threads of wax.

Funeral bundle

A body that has been arranged in a foetal position and wrapped in textiles before its burial, often accompanied by pieces of clothing and other funerary offerings.

Gilding

he process of coating an object in gold leaf or powder.

Granulation

A metalworking technique in which tiny balls of metal are applied to a metal object for decoration.

Lime dipper
A dipper consisting of a finial attached to a long stem, used to transfer the lime powder used in coca chewing from the *poporo* to the mouth.

Lost-wax casting
A process in which an object is sculpted in wax and encased in a ceramic mould. Molten metal is then poured in through a channel, melting the wax and filling the resulting cavity, creating an exact metal replica of the wax model. Hollow objects can be created using this method with the employment of an internal core. Also called lost-mould casting, *cire perdue*.

Matrix
A carved stone block with raised relief surfaces, used with the lost-wax technique to mass produce sets of identical cast elements for necklaces and figurine parts.

Monolithic
Made from a single block of stone. From Greek *monolithos* ('single stone').

Necropolis
An ancient or prehistoric burial ground, especially one with elaborate tombs. From Greek *nekropolis* ('city of the dead').

Ocarina
Italian: 'little goose'. An ancient type of wind instrument found in both Central and South America and South and East Asia, often made from terracotta, with a rounded body with finger holes from which a mouth piece protrudes.

Peccary
A pig-like mammal of the family *tayassuidae* that is found throughout most of South and Central America and parts of North America.

Pectoral
A pendant or other ornament worn suspended from the neck and resting on the chest.

Poporo
A container with a lid (often made from a gourd) that holds the lime powder that is chewed, together with coca leaves, to facilitate the absorption of stimulants.

Repoussé
French: 'pushed up'. A metalworking technique in which designs are imprinted on metal sheets by hammering their reverse sides with metal or stone tools.

Sarcophagus
A stone coffin. From Greek *lithos sarkophagos* ('flesh-eating stone').

Tejuelo
A small button-shaped piece of metal that forms at the bottom of a crucible after melting, and which can then be shaped by hammering.

Tianga
A seat (in the form of a chair or stool) used in pre-Columbian societies in ritual ceremonies, usually by a spiritual leader. Also used in a burial context in some societies with miniature versions often interred with a mummy bundle.

Tumbaga
An alloy composed of mainly gold and copper but occasionally containing other metals such as silver. Probably from Malay *tembaga* ('copper').

Tumulus
Latin: 'mound'. A burial mound or barrow.

Tunjo
A votive figure made from gold alloy using the lost-wax technique. Used by people in the Muisca region as an offering to the gods.

Yopo
Anadenanthera peregrina, a tree native to the Caribbean and South America. Its seeds have been widely used among South American indigenous societies since pre-Columbian times to produce a hallucinogenic snuff used in healing ceremonies.

Bibliography and further reading

Botero Cuerva, C. and J.-F. Bouchard. 2000. *Les Esprits, l' Or et le Chamane: Musée de l' Or de Colombie.* Paris: Réunion des Musées Nationaux

Bray, W. 1978. The Gold of El Dorado. London: Times Newspapers Ltd

Broadbent, S. 1985. 'Chibcha Textiles in the British Museum', in *Antiquity* 59 (227): 202–5

Cardale Schripff, M. (ed.). 2005. *Calima and Malagana: Art and Archaeology in Southwestern Colombia.* Bogotá: Pro Calima Foundation

Castellanos, Juan de. 1589. In Restrepo, Luis Fernando. 2004. *Antologia Critica de Juan de Castellanos. Elegías de Varones Ilustres de Indias, Historia de Nuevo Reino de Granada.* Bogotá: Editorial Pontifica Universidad Javeriana

Cieza de Léon, Pedro de. 1864. *The Travels of Piedro de Cieza de Léon, AD 1532–50, Contained in the First Part of his Chronicle of Peru* (trans. and ed. Clements R. Markham). London: Hakluyt Society, Series I, Vol. 33

De Bry, Theodor. 1599. *Historia Americae.* Frankfurt

Dillehay, T. (ed.). 2011. Tombs for the *Living: Andean Mortuary Practices.* Washington, DC: Dumbarton Oaks Research Library and Collection

Falchetti, Ana María, and Plazas de Nieto, Clemencia. 1973. *El Territorio de los Muiscas a la llegada de los Espanoles.* Bogotá: Cuadernos de Antropologia 1, Universidad de los Andes

Fischer, M. (ed.). 1994. *El Dorado. Das Gold der Fürstengräber.* Berlin: Reimer

Freyle, Juan Rodríguez. 1989. *Conquista y Descubrimiento del Nuevo Reino de Granada.* Spain: Industria Cultural

Labbé, A. and W. Bray. 1999. *Shamans, Gods, and Mythic Beasts: Colombian Gold and Ceramics in Antiquity.* New York: University of Washington Press

Labbé, A. (ed.). 2002. *Tribute to the Gods: Treasures of the Museo del Oro.* Santa Ana: The Bowers Museum of Cultural Art

Lleras Pérez, R. and C. Botero. 2007. *The Art of Gold: The Legacy of Pre-Hispanic Colombia.* Milan: Skira Editore

McEwan, C. 2009. *Ancient American Art in Detail.* London: The British Museum Press

McEwan, C. (ed.). 2000. *Precolumbian Gold: Technology, Style and Iconography.* London: The British Museum Press

Nuñez de Balboa, Vasco. 1829. *Carta dirigida al Rey por Vasco Nuñez de Balboa desde Santa María del Darien.* In de Navarrette, Martin Fernandez (ed.). *Colección de los viajes y descubrimientosque bicieron por mar los españoles desde fines del siglo.* XV. 1825–1837

Olsen, D. 2002. *Music of El Dorado: The Ethnomusicology of Ancient South American Cultures.* Gainesville: University Press of Florida

Olsen Bruhns, K. 1994. *Ancient South America.* Cambridge: University Press

Oviedo y Valdés, Gonzalez Fernández de. 1535. *Historia general y natural de Las Indias, islas y Tierra Firme del Mar Océano (General and Natural History of the Indies, Islands and Terrra Firme of the Ocean Sea)*. Madrid: Biblioteca de autores españoles, Editorial Atlas

Quilter, J. and J. Hoopes (eds). 2003. *Gold and Power in Ancient Costa Rica, Panama and Colombia*. Washington: Dumbarton Oaks

Paz Maldonado, Fray Juan de. 1582. *Relación del Pueblo de San Andrés de Xunxi, Provincia de Riobamba*. Madrid: Relaciones Histórico-Geográficas de la Audiencia de Quito (S.XVI–XIX), CSIC. T.1

Ralegh, Sir Walter. 1848. *The Discoverie of the Large, Rich and Beautiful Empire of Guiana* (1596). London: Hakluyt Society, Series I, Vol. 3

Salomon, F. and S. Schwartz. 1999. *The Cambridge History of the Native Peoples of the Americas, Vol. 3: South America, Part 1*. Cambridge: University Press

Sarmiento, Pedro. 1540. *Relacion del viaje del Capitán Jorge Robledo a las provincias de Anserma y Quimbaya (Account of the Journey by Captain Jorge Robledo to the Provinces of Anserma and Quimbaya)*

Saunders, N. 1998. Icons of Power: *Feline Symbolism in the Americas*. London: Routledge

Sardella, Juan Bautista. 1541. *Relación del descubrimiento de las provincias de Antioquia por Jorge Robledo*. In 1921 Repertorio Historico de la Academia Antioqueña de Historia

Scott, D. 2012. *Gold and Platinum Metallurgy of Ancient Colombia and Ecuador*. Los Angeles: Conservation Science Press

Silverman, H. and W. Isbell. 2008. *Handbook of South American Archaeology*. New York: Springer

Simón, Pedro. 1882–92. *Noticias Historiales de las Conquistas de Tierra Firme en las Indias Occidentales*. Bogotá

Stone, R. 2011. *The Jaguar Within: Shamanic Trance in Ancient Central and South American Art*. Austin: University of Texas Press

Illustration acknowledgements

All photographs of objects from the Museo del Oro are © Museo del Oro – Banco de la República, Colombia. Museo del Oro registration numbers are given in the captions. Further information about the Museo del Oro and its collection can be found at banrepcultural.org/gold-museum.

All photographs of objects from the British Museum are © The Trustees of the British Museum, courtesy of the Department of Photography and Imaging. British Museum registration numbers are given in the captions. Further information about the British Museum and its collection can be found at britishmuseum.org.

The sources of other illustrations are as listed below:

p. 18 © Mauricio Mejía

pp. 20–21, 22, 23, 53, 54, 57 © The British Library Board

p. 163 above © Monique & Thomas

p. 163 below © Levi in Latijns Amerika – Net Als Kuifje

p 164 © JTB Photo / SuperStock

Index

Note: page numbers in **bold** refer to information contained in captions.